D1477880

BULK CARRIERS

THE OCEAN CINDERELLAS

NICK TOLERTON

ISBN: 0-9582535-6-0

Set in Frutiger 10.5/13pt

Cover Design and Layout by Tristan Brehaut
for Willson Scott Publishing Limited
Email: design@willsonscott.biz

Cover Photograph by Nick Tolerton

Printed in China by Everbest Printing Company
through Willson Scott Publishing Limited in association with Merivale Press,
Christchurch, New Zealand
Email: publish@willsonscott.biz
www.willsonscott.biz

6

4

2

14 M

8

6

4

2

13 M

8

6

4

2

12 M

8

6

4

2

11 M

8

6

4

2

10 M

8

6

4

2

9 M

8

6

4

2

8 M

8

6

4

2

7 M

8

6

4

2

6 M

8

6

4

Cape Maxim, 1984, 149,581dwt (C Lous)

INTRODUCTION

Why bulk carriers? By gross tonnage, dry bulk carriers make up a third of the world's shipping fleet and move about three billion tonnes of cargo a year, yet surely receive less public attention than any other vehicles in the world of transport. The admiration of both shipping industry professionals, seagoing or ashore, and of shipping enthusiasts tends to be reserved for more glamorous vessels – passengers ships, container ships, cargo liners, and coasters.

Oil tankers may not be admired, but these vessels receive much greater scrutiny than the humble dry bulk carrier. Oil giants like BP and Shell are household names and their fleets have long histories. And in the event of disaster, the environmental consequences ensure front page and television lead item prominence.

In contrast bulk carrier owners, their vessels flying the flags of Liberia, Panama, or Hong Kong, are much more anonymous. Their ships, like tankers, often load and discharge their cargoes at remote terminals and berths away from public gaze. But when these vessels are victims of maritime accidents, they are less likely to be publicised. They are not at risk of spilling many thousands of tonnes of crude oil to pollute the seashore and kill wildlife. And their crews are usually third world sailors whose deaths go unnoticed.

That has changed a little since the 1980 sinking of the *Derbyshire* – the largest British vessel lost – and the Australian "Ships of Shame" inquiry after the sinking of several very large bulk carriers. But in spite of growing concern among naval architects, regulatory bodies, and classification societies about bulk carrier safety, these ships remain the Cinderellas of the seas.

When bulk carriers do feature in nautical books or publications, it is generally the ultra large vessels or exotics like the combination carriers. However, this book is unapologetically weighted towards the Panamaxs and handysize bulk carriers, plodding the oceans at 13-14 knots, that numerically make up much the largest part of the world's dry bulk fleet. They are also the types most likely to be observed by anyone with an interest in ships. And whatever else might be said about them, many of these bulkers are ships of character.

Unless she's straight from the builder or dock, you won't see a pristine bulk carrier. They are hard-worked ships, and their rusting, stained hulls invariably show that. And just as much as tankers, they are absolutely indispensable to world trade. The vessels and the sailors of all nations who man them deserve more recognition than they've had. This book certainly isn't the last word on bulk carriers, but I hope it stimulates more interest in this neglected area of shipping.

Polska Walczaca, 73,505dwt, 1992 – one of the later Burmeister & Wain Panamaxs (C Lous)

CONTENTS

CHAPTER ONE

EVOLUTION OF THE BULK CARRIER

Few phenomena in maritime history match the staggering growth of the world's dry bulk carrier fleet.

In 1964 Lloyds Register first listed ore and bulk carriers as a separate ship type in its statistics. The fleet has grown from 16,665,109 gross tons and 1304 ships that year to 38,334,465gt and 2321 ships in 1970, 83,354,613gt and 4282 ships in 1980, 113,421,003gt and 4796 ships in 1990, and 142,683,847gt (254,984,117dwt) and 4886 ships in 2000.

Iron ore, coal, and grain are the major commodities shipped by the bulk fleet, and it is grain, because of fluctuations in supply and demand and its seasonal nature, that is the historic trigger for freight rates. The world's ever-growing appetite for these commodities, as well as other significant bulk cargoes like phosphate, has spurred the growth of the bulk carrier fleet. Volumes of the major bulk commodities carried at sea considerably more than doubled in the 20 years from 1965.

Cometh the hour, cometh the ship. It is a measure of the success of the bulk carrier that in its basics this ship type has not in fact changed greatly over more than four decades. As the container ship superseded the cargo liner, the single deck bulk carrier replaced the tweendeck tramp in a shipping revolution just as important for world trade as containerisation.

UK maritime historians advance claims for two British vessels to have places of importance in the history of the bulk carrier. The little 485gt iron *John Bowes* of 1852 from the Charles Palmer yard, Jarrow, was the first screw steamer for the coal trade from the North-east to London, making the traditional Geordie brigs obsolete almost overnight. Very early in her career water ballast tanks were fitted in the bottom of her one hold, providing a tangible connection to the modern bulk ship. More forgotten by history (perhaps because her career was so brief) has been the *Silurian* of 1924 from the Blythswood yard, Glasgow. The last ship built for Cardiff owners Owen & Watkin Williams, she was a ship in advance of her day – an engines-aft vessel of about 11,000dwt and the world's largest oceangoing single-deck motorship. She was sold within three years to Furness Withy when the Williams business collapsed, but wrecked in 1928.

The ore trade has had a major role in the genesis of the bulk ship. On the North American Great Lakes the development of the bulk freighter traces back to 1869 and the launch in Cleveland of the 64m one-hold wooden steam vessel *R J Hackett* to carry iron ore.

The development of the ore trade from Scandinavia led Swedish shipping companies Axel Johnson, Axel Brostrom, and Grangesberg-Oxelosund into the development of specialised oceangoing ore carriers. Johnson's trunk steamer *Oscar Fredrik* (1900/6540dwt) was Sweden's largest ship of her day and carried ore from Lulea and Narvik to Antwerp and Rotterdam. She later pioneered Johnson's South American liner service, and subsequently had tween decks installed to make her more suitable for general cargo.

It was, Brostrom, however, that was responsible for the most significant milestone in the evolution of the bulk carrier and the bulk trades when its company A/B Tirfing took delivery of the *Amerikaland* and *Svealand* from Deutsche Werft, Hamburg, in 1925. With a deadweight of 20,600 and 174m long, the pair were the largest oceangoing cargo ships of their day, carrying iron ore from Chile via the Panama canal to the world's largest steel plant, Bethlehem Steel Co's works at Sparrows Point, Maryland. Both motorships, the pair had three holds with large spaces between them and the sides and bottom for water ballast, and nine hinged steel hatch covers raised and lowered by winches.

The two vessels were not just innovative technically. The long-term contract for large specially-designed bulk ships to shuttle ore from export port to steelworks was also a blueprint for the future. *Amerikaland* was torpedoed and sunk in 1942, but her sister did not relinquish the service until 1949 – and then operated on other ore trades before going to the breakers in 1969.

Further lessons in both the financing and design development of large bulk carriers were provided in the 1950s by the reclusive American tycoon Daniel K Ludwig. In 1950 Ludwig secured a 10-year lease on the Kure shipyard where Japan's largest warships had been built. From here, the National Bulk Carriers Inc, Kure Shipyards Division, Kobe, came a series of giant (for their day) tankers and ore carriers – the former competing with newcomers to the Onassis and Niarchos fleets as the largest supertankers.

In an era of streamlining where even the most mundane cargo vessels were attractive ships, Ludwig's oil and ore carriers were no-frills ships of notably utilitarian appearance. The *Ore Chief* of 1954 was the first of three twin-screw, steam turbine 59,580dwt ore carriers. They and the *Sinclair Petrolore* (1955/56,089dwt), a self-unloading oil-ore carrier, all went into service for Ludwig's Universe Tankships under the Liberian flag, and were followed by a dozen more large ore carriers in the 50s and early 1960s.

Ludwig was skilled at obtaining charters for his vessels, primarily tankers, before construction, and using the charter contracts to obtain bank loans to build his ships, with payment deferred until they were afloat.

In Britain in the 1950s the commissioning of a series of engines-aft ore carriers to serve the British Iron and Steel Corporation on 15 year charters gave shipowners familiarity with ships much more efficient than their traditional tweendeckers for handling bulk cargoes. The BISC ships were built in two main groups – one of about 9000dwt for working restricted ports like Port Talbot and Workington, and the other of 15,000dwt or more.

The 1953 completions *Ormsary* and *Gleddoch*, both of the 9000dwt class, were the first from this programme. Both steamers built by Lithgows, they were managed by J & J Denholm and owned by Scottish Ore Carriers. Motorships subsequently dominated this programme, with the notable exception of another Lithgows vessel completed for Denholm in 1959. The *Morar* had a gas turbine, an innovation which was not successful although she was not re-engined until after her sale in 1967.

As well as tramp owners like Denholm, the liner company Houlder Brothers & Co was prominent in this programme, operating among others six of the Port Talbot-size ships through Ore Carriers. Built in 1954-56, they were the first British ships of this size to have engines and bridge aft.

The early 1950s also saw another step forward in dry bulk shipping with the advent of raised quarter deck bulk carriers in British tramp fleets, the start of a procession of large single deck vessels that would eventually see off the tweendeck tramp (the distinction of being the last under the Red Ensign went to Rowland & Marwood's SS Co's *Egton* of 1962, which was towed to Finnish breakers in 1986 after being laid-up at Hartlepool for nearly nine years).

South Shields shipbulder John Readhead & Sons led the way with these vessels, with the motorship *Hudson Deep* for Hudson SS Co and steamer *Rookwood* for Wm France, Fenwick & Co in 1952 and the steamer *Rushwood* for France, Fenwick and motorship *Camellia* for the Stag Line in 1953. All four were self-trimming 7800dwt ships with three hatches in the quarter deck and two in the well deck, and engines aft and the bridge at the break of the quarter deck. Both Hudson and the Stag Line returned to Readhead for similar vessels in the next few years.

Amerikaland – Angf.A/B Tirfing, Sweden; Deutsche Werft, Hamburg, 1925; 26,600dwt, 174m, 9ha, 2x4800shp Algemeine-B&W. (World Ship Society)

Camellia – Stag Line (J Robinson & Sons), UK; J Readhead, South Shields, 1953; 7800dwt, 132m, 5ha, Doxford (WSS)

Morar – Scottish Ore Carriers (J & J Denholm), UK; Lithgows, Port Glasgow, 1959; 9250dwt, 130m, 5ha, 1 x 5, 2 x 1.5 der, gas turbine. (WSS)

Malmo shipyard Kockums completed a milestone vessel in 1956 with the 19,420dwt *Cassiopeia* for Stockholm owner Nordstrom & Thulin. She was the first true modern dry bulk carrier, and credit for the concept goes to a New York shipbroker, Ole Skaarup, who took his ideas to Swedish industrialist Marcus Wallenberg. The *Cassiopeia*, which cost around US$2.5 million, was 163m long, and had three holds with six wide hatches and sloping wing tanks and sloping bulkheads. The economic advantages were quickly apparent. No longer did elaborate shifting boards have to be installed in the holds for grain. Cargo-handling and trimming were transformed and turnaround in port speeded up. And the large cargo capacity, double that of types like the Liberty ships that she replaced, meant the *Cassiopeia* was more economical to operate. This ship was the prototype for a series of bulk carriers from Kockums – and indeed for similar vessels from yards elsewhere.

Dry cargo growth in the 1950s also saw some tankers converted. Several smaller Shell tankers, including some pre-war veterans, were converted to ore carriers after being sold – mainly to Spanish owners for service from West African ports to Spanish ore ports, some visiting the UK. And in the mid-60s the Kulukundis-owned London & Overseas Freighters, whose German-built 27,814dwt *Overseas Courier* of 1960 had been the largest British bulk carrier of its day, converted seven of its 1950s-built tankers, all around 25,000dwt, to bulk carriers at a time when tankers of their size were proving uneconomic.

Sea Amethyst – Stephenson Clarke Shipmanagement, UK; SA Juliana Constructora Gijonesa, Gijon, 1987; 11,901dwt, 142m, 4ha, 5248hp Bazan-MAN (C Lous)

Poles apart: Two British-operated bulk carriers at opposite extremes of size. The *Sea Amethyst* of 1987 (top) is a 11,901dwt Spanish-built, Douglas-registered ship reflecting the continuing involvement in short sea bulk shipping of Stephenson Clarke, whose ships were always prominent in North-east coal trade. She previously traded as *Cardona* and *Amethyst*. The Bermuda-registered 149,513dwt *York* of 1990 (lower) was part of P&O's bulk fleet operated by Associated Bulk Carriers from Hong Kong.

York – Associated Bulk Carriers (Zodiac Maritime Agencies), Bermuda; China Shipbuilding, Kaohsiung, 1990; 149,513dwt, 270m, 9ha, 14,370bhp Kawasaki-B&W (C Lous)

8

4

2

14 M

8

6

4

2

13 M

8

6

4

2

12 M

8

6

4

2

11 M

8

6

4

2

10 M

8

6

4

2

9 M

8

6

4

2

8 M

8

6

4

2

7 M

8

6

4

2

6 M

8

6

4

CHAPTER TWO

GROWTH AND TECHNICAL INNOVATION

Major growth in seaborne trade in the 1960s and the need for owners to replace war-built and immediate postwar dry cargo tonnage set the scene for the world's bulk carrier fleet to grow very quickly. And it was also to benefit from unique growth in trade in the six years or so from 1967, after the Six Day War and subsequent closure of the Suez Canal. As with the tanker fleet, larger and larger bulk carriers were launched, and by the end of the 1960s 100,000dwt bulk carriers and ore carriers and considerably larger combination carriers were in service.

However, while the largest new vessels, as with tankers, drew the most attention, it was handysize and Panamax bulkers that numerically dominated the world fleet. And the basic features of these types have changed little in the ensuing half century since the *Cassiopeia* was launched.

Thus the typical self-trimming bulk carrier: An engine-aft, singledeck ship, with topside wing tanks and hopper bilge tanks that can be used for ballast (the inclined sides of the latter also facilitating discharge of the cargo), and double bottom tanks that can be used for ballast or fuel.

Although many of the characteristics of these ships have not changed, there has been evolution. Perhaps the main improvement has come in more efficient engines, fuel economy being an understandable obsession with both owners and builders which received particularly close attention after the oil shocks of the 1970s.

Within the handysize and Panamax categories that dominate the world bulk carrier fleet numerically, there has also been a steady growth in size. The typical handysize bulker of the 1960s-1970s was a ship of much less than 30,000dwt, while today vessels classed as handysize typically range to 46,000dwt, and in recent years the new category of handymaxs (up to 55,000dwt) has evolved. More powerful cranes have become standard – early crane-fitted handysize bulk carriers had 8 and 10tn cranes while today 30 and 35tn cranes are usual.

The Panamax bulk carrier (usually gearless) is wedded to a 32m beam restriction for the Panama Canal, but here, too, there has been a steady sizing upwards. The latest Panamaxs are typically ships of 75,000dwt compared with under 60,000dwt for the early Panamaxs of similar dimensions.

Above the Panamaxs come the Capesize bulk carriers, typically of about 170,000dwt and 289m long, but many ore carriers are considerably larger than that. The biggest bulk carrier is the 343m long Bergesen ore carrier *Berge Stahl* (1986/364,767dwt), built by Hyundai Heavy Industries, Ulsan.

The *Berge Stahl* was followed in the Bergesen fleet in 1992 by the 322,941dwt *Bergeland* (also from Hyundai) with the distinction of being the world's second-largest ore carrier. A more recent giant of note was the seven-hatch 322,398dwt ore carrier *Peene Ore* of 1997 from Daewoo, which went into service on a 10 year charter carrying Australian and South African iron ore to Rotterdam for Krupp. She's operated by F Laeisz of Hamburg – a far cry from the famous sailing ships of

Skaufast – A/S Eikland (I M Skaugen & Co), Norway; Harland & Wolff, Belfast, 1968; 99,800dwt, 261m, 9ha, 20,700bhp H&W. (APN)

The 99,800dwt *Skaufast*, going down the slipway at Harland & Wolff, Belfast, in August 1968, was hailed as the largest bulk carrier built in Europe when she was launched.

Laeisz's "Flying P" fleet. Pure ore carriers have two longitudinal bulkheads creating very large wing ballast tanks, and a deep double bottom, the ore being carried only in the centre holds.

The largest bulk carriers invariably operate on long-term charters shipping ore or coal, and many operate for the Japanese shipping giants NYK, Mitsui OSK, and Kawasaki carrying ore and coal to meet the demands of that country's steel and power companies.

The two constituents of Mitsui OSK Lines, today the world's largest operator of bulk carriers, were both active in ore carrying before their 1964 merger. OSK built its first ore carrier, the *Harriet Maru* (28,182dwt), in 1962 to a 15-year cargo guarantee from Sumitomo Metal Industries. The ship, shuttling between Canada and Sumitomo's Wakayama steelworks, was the world's largest ore carrier, and started a close relationship between OSK and Sumitomo which continued after the merger. Mitsui had a similar association with Yawata Iron & Steel (which later merged with Fuji to form Nippon Steel) begun with the 1960 ore carriers *Yashiwosan Maru* (18,486dwt) and *Yawatasan Maru* (27,056dwt), both also built on 15-year cargo guarantees.

The merged Mitsui OSK had ships operating for all the major Japanese steel makers, and reached another milestone in 1970 with Japan's largest ore carrier, the 123,744dwt *Yachiyosan Maru,* built to a cargo guarantee from Nippon Steel.

Japan's other giant, Nippon Yusen Kaisha, was just as quick to develop links with industry for long term contracts. Its first ore carrier was the *Tobata Maru* (20,989dwt), built in 1960 jointly for NYK and Toho Kaiun to carry ore from Zungun, Malaysia, and Goa for Yawata, and fitted with 10 5tn derricks. Two years later came the first of the modern-style ore carriers for NYK, the 50,752dwt *Okitsu Maru,* a gearless 10-hatch ship built on a contract to carry iron ore from Long Beach for four steel companies. With world crude steel production growing at about 4% a year and Japan's at about 6.5%, there was a corresponding need for ships of this type, and NYK added seven large ore carriers to its fleet in 1963-66. At 111,230dwt, the nine-hatch *Chikuho Maru* of 1975, built to carry coal from Australia and Canada for Nippon Steel but also reinforced for ore, was another milestone for NYK.

These ships continued to grow in size. The *Shin Ogishima Maru* of 1981, built to replace two of the mid-60s vessels, was 194,109dwt. She was designed with shallow draught (18.2m) and wide beam (50m), and energy-saving features including a low fuel consumption, low speed Burmeister & Wain 23,900bhp engine. This ship's usual service was carrying iron ore from Port Dampier to Kawasaki. Another very large ship, the 198,906dwt *Onga Maru* of 1985, took energy-saving concerns a step further by the incorporation of air resistance-reducing vanes on either side of her superstructure.

Ships were built not only to serve the steel industry on guaranteed cargo contracts. They were also built, particularly in the last 25 years, to cargo guarantees from power companies. NYK's shallow draught, wide-beam *Saikai Maru* (70,407dwt) of 1980, was Japan's first coal carrier built to carry steaming coal for use in electricity generation, and carried cargoes from Australia and South Africa to a thermal power plant. Another NYK ship, the *Shiromine Maru* (92,067dwt) of 1982 was the first coal carrier built with a long-term cargo guarantee with both a steel company and a power company. Running from Australia, she carried coking coal for steel-making and steaming coal for power generation, loaded in separate hatches.

Another NYK bulker, the 91,443dwt *Noshiro Maru* of 1993, was claimed as the first double skin coal carrier, built to carry Australian coal to Tokyo Electric power stations. She is a completion from Oshima Shipbuilding, which has been a pioneer in double hull bulker construction.

As well as helping domestic owners, Japan's volcanic growth also created opportunities which helped Hong Kong owners like Y K Pao (World-Wide) and T Y and Frank Chao (Wah Kwong) vault to prominence.

Bulk carrier construction, of course, played its part in the Japanese shipbuilding boom which saw Japan rise to world preeminence last century, and Japanese shipyards were quick to offer portfolios of standard designs.

Japanese construction of the largest bulk carriers, like super tankers, has been dominated by its big seven builders: Hitachi Zosen, Ishikawajima-Harima Heavy Industries, Kawasaki Heavy

Rila – Navigation Maritime Bulgare, Bulgaria; Georgi Dimitrov Shipyard, Varna, 1977; 25,926dwt, 185m, 7ha, 12,000bhp Cegielski-Sulzer. (C Lous)

Series building has been the norm for bulk carrier construction at Asian and East European shipyards. The 25,926dwt *Rila* of 1977 (above) is one of a long series of similar ships from Bulgaria's Georgi Dimitrov Shipyard, Varna, and part of the fleet of state owner Navigation Maritime Bulgare. In contrast the contribution of United States shipyards to the ocean-going bulk carrier fleet has been small, although the *Judy Litrico* (below) is one. The twin-engined 29,984dwt ship was completed in 1973 by Lockheed, Seattle, as the *Sugar Islander* and in 1996 changed name to firstly *Islander* and then *Judy Litrico*.

Judy Litrico – Gulfcoast Transit Co, USA; Lockheed Shipbuilding & Construction Co, Seattle, 1973; 29,984dwt, 195m, 6ha, 12,000bhp 2 x Pielstick. (Kevin Moore)

Tachibana – Powercoal Navigation Corp (MOL Shipmanagement Asia Pte), Panama; Koyo Dockyard, Mihara, 2000; 154,324dwt, 274m, 7ha, 19,168hp Mitsui-B&W. (JSEA)

The 154,324dwt coal carrier *Tachibana*, completed in 2000 for Mitsui OSK by Koyo Dockyard, is typical of the larger bulk carriers in service today. Mitsui OSK is the biggest operator of bulk carriers, and many of its ships like this vessel are built against supply contracts from Japanese power companies and steelworks.

Iron Curtis – BHP Transport, Australia; Whyalla Shipbuilding & Engineering Works, Whyalla, 1978; 45,428dwt, 202m, 7ha, 10,902bhp 2 x Wartsila. (Tolerton)

Diesel propulsion is universal for bulk carriers – almost. One of the exceptions was the *Iron Curtis* of 1978 for Australia's Broken Hill Proprietary, which like her sister *Iron Carpentaria* of 1977 had an 8542kw General Electric gas turbine. Ongoing problems led to both being re-engined with twin Wartsila diesels. The *Curtis* was the last ship built at Whyalla Shipyard.

Industries, Mitsubishi Heavy Industries, Mitsui Engineering & Shipbuilding, NKK Corporation (formerly Nippon Kokan), and Sumitomo Heavy Industries. Hitachi and NKK merged in 2002 to form Universal Shipbuilding Corporation, Japan's second-largest builder behind Mitsubishi.

The elite seven and the four other listed builders (Naikai Zosen, Namura Shipbuilding, Sanoyas Hishino Meisho, and Sasebo Heavy Industries) have also been to the fore in the construction of smaller bulkers, but outside them several companies in the so-called "second tier" of Japanese shipbuilding like Oshima Shipbuilding, Hakodate Dock, and Tsuneishi Zosen have specialised in bulk carrier construction – some of them almost exclusively.

If outwardly and internally the bulk carrier has probably changed less than most ship types over its half century serving world trade, it has nevertheless been the subject of some experimentation. Some of the most interesting has been in Australian fleets, with coal-fired steamers and gas turbine propulsion.

The Australian National Line's 76,308dwt ore carrier *River Boyne* of 1982 was the world's first new coal-fired steamer for more than quarter of a century – but rather different than the "dirty British steamer" of the past. Built by Mitsubishi, she had two Mitsubishi steam turbines, and twin boilers which were fed lump coal pneumatically from two main bunkers abaft the engineroom, with a combined capacity of 3000tn.

She and her sister the *River Embley* which entered service in 1983 were built to carry bauxite from Weipa to Gladstone (both in Queensland) – a 2500 miles round voyage. Environmental protections were a special concern for a ship operating near the Great Barrier Reef, and the ash was discharged in a water slurry.

Two more coal-fired bulkers, the 75,105dwt *TNT Capricornia* and *TNT Carpentaria* (both from Italcantieri in 1983), were also built for the Weipa-Gladstone bauxite run.

Australia's biggest company, Broken Hill Proprietary, experimented differently with its *Iron Carpentaria* of 1977 and *Iron Curtis* of 1978. It opted for General Electric gas turbines for this 45,432dwt pair, both built to carry coal from Gladstone to BHP's Whyalla steelworks by Whyalla Shipbuilding. The gas turbines were not successful, and both ships were re-engined with twin Wartsila medium speed diesels, returning to service in 1984.

In Japan, experimentation took a different avenue in the 1980s with auxiliary sails to try to achieve fuel economies. The first large ocean-going ship specially designed with sail-assisted propulsion was the 26,666dwt bulker *Usuki Pioneer* of 1984 from Usuki Tekkosho. The ship had two 16m high 20m wide computer-controlled aerofoil sails set on two of the crane pedestals above the booms so as not to interfere with cargo handling, and it was hoped the sails, combined with other energy-saving features, would provide fuel savings of 15 to 40 per cent. Another pioneer sail-assisted bulk carrier, the 31,217dwt *Aqua City*, was also completed in 1984, by Nippon Kokan. Her sails were removed two years later, but after several changes of name the *Usuki Pioneer* apparently retained her sails well into the 1990s.

Later in the 1980s in Britain, Stephenson Clarke's small bulker *Ashington* (1979/6570dwt) was the subject of a two-year experiment with an auxiliary wingsail.

In hull design one of the significant developments of recent years has been NKK's axe bow, introduced on the 172,564dwt Capesize *Kohyohsan* of 2001. The ship won that year's Society of Naval Architects of Japan Ship of the Year award, and several more NKK bulkers with this feature quickly followed. The sharp-edged axe bow, named for the bow shape, is intended to reduce resistance in rougher seas, whereas previous design refinement in this area has tended to focus on performance in ideal sea conditions. A reduction in fuel oil consumption of about four per cent was claimed.

An innovative bulker of quite a different type is Canadian operator Fednav's *Arctic* of 1978, a 29,450dwt OBO built by Port Weller Dry Docks and the only icebreaker bulk carrier of this size in the world. The vessel was ordered as a joint venture of the federal government and private companies, and bought by Fednav in 1996, nowadays carrying nickel concentrate from Deception Bay to Quebec City.

4

2

14 M

8

6

4

2

13 M

8

6

4

2

12 M

8

6

4

2

11 M

8

6

4

2

10 M

8

6

4

2

9 M

8

6

4

2

8 M

8

6

4

2

7 M

8

6

4

2

6 M

8

6

4

CHAPTER THREE

BRITISH LINER COMPANIES IN BULK SHIPPING

Many traditional British liner companies experimented in dry bulk shipping when changing trade patterns and the advent of container shipping, with its enormous capital costs, forced them to diversify. It was to be an unhappy experience for most. They entered this sector in the 1960s and early 1970s only to be king-hit by the depressed rates later this decade and even worse in the 80s for which they were ill-equipped to compete with the flag of convenience fleets. British pay scales, manning scales, and traditional standards of maintenance were a burden competing against operators who were much more economical in these areas.

Even the grandest British company of all, Cunard, ordered eight humble standard design bulk carriers, 27,000dwt Euskalduna 27s from the Seville yard of Astilleros Espanoles SA in a 20 million pound construction programme. The first, the *Cunard Campaigner* of 1972, was followed by the *Cunard Caravel*, *Cunard Carronade*, *Cunard Calamanda*, *Cunard Cavalier*, *Cunard Carrier*, *Cunard Champion*, and *Cunard Chieftain*. Seven-hatch vessels with four 15tn cranes, all were delivered in 1972-73, and operated in Brocklebank funnel colours. However, the first two were quickly sold in 1974 to India's Great Eastern Shipping Co, and before 1979 all had been sold.

The famous funnel colours of another member of the British elite, Blue Funnel, also appeared on bulk carriers in the 1970s. The Ocean group's attempts to diversify at this time seemed to be particularly ill-fated. Their gas tanker *Nestor* of 1977 must have been one of the most disastrous investments any British shipping company made, and although the bulk carriers did not lose Ocean as much money, they did not fulfill the company's hopes. Some of Blue Funnel's most famous names were revived for a group of five 27,000dwt ships delivered from Mitsui Shipbuilding & Engineering Co in 1972-73 – the *Achilles*, *Agamemnon*, *Antenor*, *Anchises*, and *Ajax*, six-hatch vessels with five 8tn cranes. Much of their trading was to the Great Lakes. Like the Cunard ships, their careers with their famous owners were not lengthy. Coincidentally the *Cunard Carrier* came under Ocean management as the *Aeneas* after a Hong Kong owner acquired her in 1978.

Ocean went into even larger bulk carriers with the *Helenus* and *Hector* of 1973, both gearless 51,000dwt Panamax ships from Burmeister & Wain, Copenhagen. The former was converted into a vehicle carrier in 1978 for a five-year charter and sold in 1983, and the latter sold in 1979. The biggest Blue Funnel bulker was the 218,035dwt ore-oil *Tantalus* of 1972.

Of the traditional liner companies which operated bulk carriers, perhaps only P&O could count the move a long term success – but even here it was not a sector which was a big earner for P&O. A December 2003 statement that it had sold its last interest in bulk shipping ended 40 years for P&O in dry bulk shipping, mainly operating large ore and combination carriers.

P&O took delivery of its first bulk carrier in 1965, after it and Erling Naess's Anglo Norness Shipping Co set up Associated Bulk Carriers for joint operation of their bulkers the previous year. In 1971 the P&O Bulk Shipping Division was created to take over management of the group's

Cunard Champion – Cunard SS Co (Cunard Brocklebank Bulkers), UK; Astilleros Espanoles, Bilbao, 1973; 26,646dwt, 183m, 7ha, 4 x 15tn cr, 9900bhp Ast.Espanoles-Sulzer. (Tolerton)

Cunard went into bulk shipping with eight Euskalduna 27 standard designs from Astilleros Espanoles, like the *Cunard Champion* (above). As well as four cranes, she had two prominent 1.5tn derricks aft. She was sold to the Philippines in 1978, becoming *El Champion* for Eddie Litonjua Shipping Co. P&O's move into bulk shipping was more ambitious and large-scale than its famous British rival's. The 154,907dwt *Jedforest* (below) of 1972 from Eriksbergs was one of P&O's many ore-bulk-oil carriers. Sold to Cypriot owners in 1987, she was severely damaged that year in an attack by Iraqi aircraft during the Iran-Iraq war.

Jedforest – P&O Steam Navigation Co (P&O Bulk Shipping Div), UK; Eriksbergs, Gothenburg, 1972; 154,907dwt, 291m, 11 holds/tanks, 30,400bhp Eriksbergs-B&W. (World Ship Society)

bulkers, combinations carriers, tankers, and gas tankers. The first bulk carrier had been the 43,628dwt *Atherstone* from Hitachi Zosen in 1965 – starting the style of naming P&O's bulkers and combination carriers after fox hunts. Within two years the 73,000dwt OBOs *Eridge*, *Grafton*, and *Heythrop* had been added, and by the time the bulk division was set up P&O had nine large bulkers and OBOs with five more on order.

The Associated Bulk Carriers title was resurrected and, Hong Kong-based, it started the new century operating 22 ships. However, P&O had long been eager to divest itself of its interest in bulkers, and finally did so when its remaining 50 per cent interest in ABC was sold to partner Eurotower Bulk Carriers at the end of 2003, when the fleet numbered five owned and seven leased and chartered Capesize bulkers. Eurotower and Zodiac Maritime, which had managed the ABC fleet for three years, are both owned by the Israeli Ofer group. Before this link in 2000, P&O had had a Chinese company as a partner in ABC for two years.

The Ben Line moved into bulk carriers by buying Hunting & Son's 28,836dwt *Wearfield* (renamed *Benhiant*) and Bolton Steam Shipping Co's 30,309dwt *Ribera* (renamed *Benvorlich*) in 1973, and considerably expanded its interest in this sector – again by shopping on Tyneside – with the acquisition of the Sheaf Steam Shipping Co and its associated Bamburgh Shipping Co in 1976, which added six bulk carriers. Ben's biggest ship was the nine-hold, 150,661dwt *Bencruachan*, delivered from Daewoo in 1983. She began her career with a two year charter to Bocimar, and was sold in 1986 as Ben Line faded out of shipping.

The British and Commonwealth group was involved in bulkers through its tramp arm, the King Line. B&C started with two ships bought while fitting out, the 77,800dwt *Elbe Ore* at Burmeister & Wain in 1967 (placed in Scottish Tanker Co ownership) and a 54,250dwt ship at Eriksbergs in 1968 which was named *King Alfred* – her third name before she left the shipyard. In 1970-75 King Line added four Panamaxs from Astilleros Espanoles.

As mentioned earlier, the Furness Withy group through Houlder had been one of the participants in the 1950s ore carrier-building programme for British Steel. Later it contributed several bulk and combination carriers to the Seabridge consortium. The largest, the OBO *Furness Bridge* (1971/168,728dwt), was the first of the class of six ill-fated ships from Swan Hunter Shipbuilders that culminated in Bibby Line's *Derbyshire*, which was lost in 1980. The company withdrew from Seabridge in 1977.

British Steel introduced a new generation of bulk carriers to supply its plants with the 118,750dwt *Abbey* of 1979, 173,028dwt *British Steel* of 1984, and 172,810dwt *Ironbridge* of 1987, and Furness Withy managed these ships. *Abbey* came from Uddevallavarvet and the latter two from Harland & Wolff.

The China Navigation Co also became a bulk carrier owner when the John Swire group diversified into new ventures, acquiring its first, the IHI-built 39,280dwt *Eredine* in 1968. In 1994 it increased its rather modest involvement in this sphere by taking delivery of a Capesize, the 163,554dwt *Erradale* – the first completion by Harland & Wolff to its S162 design, a nine-hold vessel with a number of strengthening features to address safety concerns about large bulk carriers.

Swire's great rival hong, Jardine, Matheson & Co, followed it into dry bulk shipping in the 1970s and came to operate a much larger fleet. Jardines was very active in creating joint ventures, with both eastern owners including Frank Chao's Wah Kwong Shipping and the Tung group and European owners like Salen, Bocimar, and the Gearbulk consortium companies among its many partners. Through Jardine Ship Management and IndoChina Ship Management in Hong Kong, Jardine has remained prominent in bulk shipping into a new century.

T & J Harrison was another to try its luck operating bulk carriers in the 1970s. The Liverpool company had three handysize bulkers and two Panamaxs, but the former were sold 1986-88 after the larger pair had been sold in 1983. The *Wayfarer*, *Wanderer*, and *Warrior* were 1973 completions from Nippon Kokan, 27,571dwt, 15.5kn ships with six holds and five 8tn cranes, costing three million pounds each and delivered to operate for Atlantic Bulkers. The W class trio was followed by the *Specialist* and *Strategist* of 1975, two early completions at nine million pounds each by Burmeister & Wain to its 60,900dwt Panamax standard design.

Harrison's *Warrior* (above) and *Wayfarer* (below), two of a 1973 trio from Nippon Kokan's Shimizu yard, took the famous Liverpool company's "two of fat and one of lean" funnel colours to new waters. They and their sister *Wanderer* were sold in 1986-88. The *Wanderer*, which had an unlucky career for mishaps, had one too many in 1999 when as the *Ocean Wave* she stranded and broke up, and her sisters went to the breakers in 1999.

Wayfarer and *Warrior* – Charente SS Co (T & J Harrison), UK; Nippon Kokan, Shimizu, 1973; 27,571dwt, 174m, 6ha, 5 x 8tn cr, 12,000bhp Sumitomo-Sulzer. (both Tolerton)

As well as these five ships, Harrison have operated the handysize bulkers *Lantau Trader*, *Lamma Forest*, *Pisces Pioneer*, *Pisces Planter*, *Pisces Explorer*, and *Pisces Trader* through associated Hong Kong companies.

Harrison's five owned bulk carriers brought its famous "two of fat and one of lean" funnel and red Maltese cross houseflag to many ports where it was unfamiliar. The three Ws, for example, were on the phosphate run to New Zealand. Some of the Harrison bulk carrier voyages from the early 1980s are detailed below – and they also illustrate why the managers at companies like Harrison must have pined for the relative certainties of their conventional liner service days:

Wayfarer – Bagged barley, Lattakia to Bandar Abbas. Month's delay because of cargo infestation requiring fumigation. Ballast to Durban for further fumigation and alternator repairs. Steel products and zircon sands, from Richards Bay, Maputo, and Port Elizabeth to Port Kelang, Manila, Moji, Nagoya, Kawasaki. Urea, Kenai to Poro Point and Iloilo via Yokohama for bunkers (delayed at Poro Point after damage to pier while berthing). Phosphate, Nauru to Australia.

Wanderer – Coal, Port Kembla to Visakhapatnam and Haldia (after five weeks anchored at Kembla waiting for berth). To Singapore for bunkers, crew change, and repairs to damage at Haldia locks. Coal, Port Kembla to Paradip. To Singapore for bunkers and orders. To anchorage Port Kembla seeking cargo. Idle six weeks. Alumina, Gladstone to Kitimat. Vancouver, for orders. Strike-bound two weeks. Wheat, Portland to Dammam/Jeddah.

Warrior – Ballast, Bluff to Port Kembla. Strike delays at Kembla. Coal, to India. Bunkers, Singapore. Fixed for phosphate, Nauru to Bunbury, Kwinana, and Geraldton. Unable to berth at Nauru for nearly two months because of bad weather and had to divert to Honiara for diesel oil, freshwater, and provisions. (Nauru to Australia took 118 days.) Alumina, Kwinana to Richards Bay.

Specialist – Corn, Reserve to Chiba, Kawasaki, and Kashima. Ballasted unfixed in Pacific, for Australian or west coast US cargo options. Corn, Mississippi to Kashima and Kobe. Drifted off Japanese coast awaiting orders. Ordered towards Singapore. Coal, Newcastle (NSW) to eastern Mediterranean, via Adelaide for engine repairs and Fremantle for bunkers. To Norfolk for grain, sorghums, or soybeans for Japan.

Strategist – Idle more than a month at Sydney because of port congestion through industrial disputes. To Le Havre, via Capetown for bunkers and Freetown for crew change. Ordered towards Key West unfixed. Grain, US Gulf to Nagoya and Kobe, via Long Beach for bunkers. Machinery damage discovered while at Long Beach and delayed a week for repairs. Breakdown two days from Japan. To Ulsan for docking and repairs after cargo discharge.

Lantau Trader – Furnace slag, Fos to Depranon. Urea, Yuzhnyy to Singapore. Ballast to Christmas Island. Phosphate, Christmas Island to Tauranga and New Plymouth. Bunkers, Sydney. Coal, Port Kembla to Visakhapatnam. Bunkers, Singapore. Phosphate, Christmas Island to Tauranga, Whangarei, and Napier (explosion in a mast house approaching Tauranga). Coal, Port Kembla to Paradip.

Another Liverpool company which had a particularly interesting involvement in bulk carriers was the Bibby Line. It operated an eclectic fleet of 14 OBOs and bulk carriers from its first in 1967 to disposal of the last, the *Berkshire*, at the end of 1983. That came three years after the disappearance of the OBO *Derbyshire* with the loss of 44 lives – the largest British ship ever lost. The *Derbyshire* tragedy is examined later in this book.

Bibby's first bulk carriers were the *Pacific Bridge* and *Atlantic Bridge* (later renamed *Dorsetshire*), 79,000dwt ships delivered in 1967 and 1968 respectively from IHI, Aioi to operate in the Seabridge consortium. Bibby eventually contributed seven more Seabridge ships. Set up in 1965 to operate large bulk carriers, Seabridge had Bibby, Bowring SS Co, H Clarkson, Furness Withy (Houlder Bros), Britain SS Co, and Silver Line as participants.

In 1970-71 three 32,280dwt car-carrying bulk carriers from Doxford & Sunderland's North Sands yard joined the fleet. The *Berkshire, Cheshire*, and *Oxfordshire* were equipped with derricks and had retractable decks for vehicle cargoes – a specialty for some bulk carriers at this time before the development of the pure car carrier. The trio were chartered long-term to Wallenius and later traded by Bibby on the open market, the car decks of the former two being removed in 1979. This pair served Bibby until 1983, but the *Oxfordshire* was sold in 1978.

The generally very difficult times in both dry bulk and oil in the mid-late 1970s and early 80s hurt Bibby, which had to lay-up its Seabridge ships when it left the consortium in 1977. Six OBOs and bulk carriers were sold in 1978-79, and after the loss of the *Derbyshire* in 1980, Bibby must have been relieved to quit this sector.

The following list of voyages of Bibby ships at the end of the 70s and early 80s shows some typical trading in this company's latter days in bulk shipping.

Derbyshire (OBO) – Reactivated from lay-up in Stavanger. Bulk cargo voyages Sept-Iles to Baltimore, then Norfolk and Saldanha Bay to Japan, then oil, Indonesia to Trinidad. Iron ore, Tubarao to Bakar. Coal from Hampton Roads and iron ore from Sepetiba Bay to Japan. Round-voyage Australia-Japan, then docked Sasebo. Coal, Hay Point to Fos. Ballast to Sept-Iles (bunkering at New York), then iron ore for Kawasaki. Off-port call at Capetown. Lost in Typhoon Orchid off Okinawa on September 9 or 10, 1980.

Berkshire (handysize) – Round-voyage Sweden-South Africa-Europe on Safmarine time-charter. Fertiliser, USA to Brazil. South Africa to Europe. Ballast to USA. Grain, US Gulf to Brazil. Drydock Capetown four weeks to repair bottom damage sustained 14 months earlier. Coal and maize, South Africa to Hamburg. Then US Gulf-Brazil-Rotterdam. Grain, Mississippi to Egypt.

Cambridgeshire (Panamax) – Dry-dock, Hong Kong (largest vessel repaired at Hong Kong United yard, Whampoa). Bauxite, Weipa to Porto Vesme. Grain, US Gulf to Japan. Coal, Newcastle (NSW) to Antwerp...Sulphur, Vancouver to South Africa via Cape Horn. Coal, Richards Bay to Mobile...Coal, Newcastle to Nippo (two voyages). Bauxite, Weipa to Japan.

Northamptonshire (handysize) Timber, Philippines and Malaysia to Liverpool (Ben Line charter). Steel products, Europe-USA. Sold and handed over to new owners, Antwerp, February 8, 1980, as *Andaman Sea*.

Dorsetshire (Panamax) – Iron ore, Narvik to continental North Europe ports (several voyages). Grain, USA to Russia (several weeks off Novorossiysk awaiting berth). Off-port call Gibraltar, crew change. Coal, Baltimore to Lulea. Iron ore, Lulea to Dunkirk. Ballast to Hampton Roads. Coal, to Taranto.

The *Cambridgeshire*, incidentally, was one of the early victims of a new maritime hazard. Lengthy delays on a 1980 voyage from Vancouver to southern Africa with sulphur resulted in hundreds of tonnes of steelwork having to be renewed when serious corrosion was found after the cargo was discharged.

The final Bibby voyaging of the *Berkshire* (the company's last bulk carrier) and *Cheshire*, both sold in 1983 when hire rates were often not meeting running costs, and the *Dorsetshire*, sold in 1982, were as follows:

Berkshire – Discharged wheat, Shuaiba (after three month wait). Hull-cleaning, Dubai. Ballast, to Richards Bay, then coal to Venice. Ballast across Atlantic (Bermuda for bunkers after sustained bad weather). Coal, Newport News to Palermo. Lay-up, Yorkhill Quay, Glasgow. Dry-dock, Falmouth. Potash, Hamburg to Capetown and Durban. Maize, to Japan. Timber, Taiwan and Philippines to South Africa. Rutile sand and grain, to Antwerp and Rotterdam. Ballast, to New Orleans. Grain, to Alexandria (one month delay before discharge, port congestion). Cement, Alcanar to Saudi Arabia (two voyages). Ballast, Yanbu to Philadelphia. Grain, to Alexandria (four weeks delay again). Cement, Alcanar to Alexandria. Towards Gibraltar, for orders. Steel and general cargo, Sao Sebastiao (lengthy delays) and Rio de Janeiro to Hong Kong, Shanghai, Tsingtao, and Hsinkang. Dry-dock Hong Kong and handed-over to new owners on December 30, 1983, and renamed *Searanger*.

Cheshire – Knock-down cars, Japan to South Africa. Dry-dock, Capetown. Grain, Durban to Japan, then CKDs, to South Africa. Coal, to South Korea. Lay-over at Ulsan awaiting charter, then ballast to Gove. Alumina, Gove to Safaga. Ballast to East London: Maize, to Japan. Bulk pitch and CKDs, to South Africa. Ballast, Capetown to East London. Maize, to Taiwan. Repairs, Kaohsiung. Sugar, Mourilyan to Malaysia. Ballast, Penang to Geraldton. Grain, Western Australia to Iskenderun. To Syros, for maintenance. Ballast, towards Gibraltar for orders. Wheat, Houston

• *Dorsetshire* – Bibby Freighters (Bibby Bros & Co), UK; IHI, Aioi, 1968; 80,807dwt, 246m, 9ha,18,400bhp IHI-Sulzer. (World Ship Society) • *Cheshire* – Britain SS Co (Bibby Bros & Co), UK; Doxford & Sunderland, North Sands, 1971; 32,280dwt, 182m, 14 x 10tn der, 15,000bhp Doxford. (World Ship Society) • *Resource 1* – International Resources Investment Inc, Panama; Doxford & Sunderland, North Sands, 1970; 32,280dwt, 182m, 7ha, 14 x 10tn der, 14,999bhp Doxford. (Tolerton)

In its 17 years in dry bulk shipping, the Bibby group operated an interesting fleet. The 80,807dwt *Dorsetshire* (top), completed in 1968 as the *Atlantic Bridge* and renamed in 1977, was one of a pair from IHI that introduced bulk carriers to the fleet, and her career spanned nearly the duration of Bibby's involvement in dry bulk shipping .The *Cheshire* of 1971 (centre), seen here in Wallenius colours and with her car decks stacked on deck, was one of a Doxford 32,000dwt trio which included the *Berkshire* (bottom), pictured laid-up at Hong Kong in 1997 as the Panamanian *Resource 1*.

to Aqaba. To Gibraltar, then Antwerp bagged grain to Jeddah. To Chalkis and handover to new owners November 2, 1983. Renamed *Maria*.

Dorsetshire – Ballast, Ghent to Baltimore. Coal, to Japan, via Panama Canal. Ballast, Kawasaki to Richards Bay. Coal, to Japan. Coal, Newcastle (NSW) to Hirohata. Coal, Newcastle to Japan. Ballast, Sakaide to Siracha. Tapioca, to Amsterdam, Bremen, and Nordenham. Awaited orders off Weser Light, then anchorage off Falmouth. Sold to Greek owners. Pre-sale drydocking, Malta. Handed over at Piraeus November 23, 1982, and renamed *Perinthos*.

That pioneer multinational Canadian Pacific is also appropriate to include here. It set up Canadian Pacific (Bermuda) in 1964 to operate oceangoing bulk vessels, and took delivery of three open hatch forest product carriers from Mitsubishi – the *H R MacMillan* (below) and *J V Clyne* in 1968 and *N R Crump* in 1969. From 1970 to 1980 the company developed a significant and eclectic fleet including handysizes (all with *Fort*) names, Panamaxs, and larger ships, as well as the open hatch ships and tankers. The difficult times of the 80s led it to quit dry bulk shipping in 1988.

H R MacMillan – Canadian Pacific (Bermuda), UK; Mitsubishi, Hiroshima, 1968; 29,513dwt, 181m, 12ha, 3 x 18tn gantry cr, 10,500bhp Mitsubishi-Sulzer. (APN)

4

2

14 M

8

6

4

2

13 M

8

6

4

2

12 M

8

6

4

2

11 M

8

6

4

2

10 M

8

6

4

2

9 M

8

6

4

2

8 M

8

6

4

2

7 M

8

6

4

2

6 M

8

6

4

CHAPTER FOUR

SCOTTISH SHIP MANAGEMENT

Bulk carriers must have appeared a heaven-sent opportunity to British tramp owners at a time when their fleets, rebuilt after the war, were aging and the role of their conventional ships as vehicles for carrying bulk cargoes was disappearing fast. However, the tramp companies proved no more immune than the liner companies to the market difficulties that afflicted their more glamorous shipping brethren when they branched into dry bulk cargo carrying.

No British tramp companies made a more determined bid for success in the dry bulk trades than long-established Glasgow owners Lyle Shipping Co and H Hogarth & Sons. They formed Scottish Ship Management in May 1968 with a share capital of 10,000 pounds, divided equally, to manage their handysize vessels although ownership of the two fleets remained separate. It was an enterprising commitment for two conservative companies – Hogarth was probably the last British company to commission conventional tweendeck steamers, finishing with the *Baron Ogilvy*, *Baron Inchcape*, and *Baron Berwick*, all of 1956, while the Lyle history "From Cape to Cape" records that when the board wanted to build a ship in the mid-1950s with engines and bridge aft, two senior masters successfully insisted it would make the ship very unmanageable docking.

At a time when bulk carriers were looking increasingly attractive to tramp owners, British government measures also provided them with incentives. In 1963 the Conservative government introduced its shipbuilding credit scheme offering 80 per cent loans to assist the ailing UK shipbuilding industry, and companies received another leg-up with the Labour government's introduction of investment grants for new ships. They did not have to be built at a British yard, and the well-documented problems at UK yards in this era encouraged UK ship owners to forsake their traditional loyalties to domestic builders and shop overseas.

Both Lyle and Hogarth had had experience with bulk carriers before SSM was created. Hogarth's first, the *Baron Inverforth*, was completed by Austin & Pickersgill in 1965, while Lyle had three ore carriers from Lithgows starting with the *Cape Franklin* of 1959, and, like Hogarth, received its first bulk carrier, the *Cape Rodney* (also from Lithgows), in 1965.

SSM was expected to provide significant economies and greater operational flexibility in a very competitive shipping sphere, and record profits recorded by Lyle from 1969 to 1974 indicate this was certainly achieved in SSM's early years. Lambert Bros of London also joined the SSM consortium early on, remaining until 1976.

Although SSM was not destined to have a long history, it operated three notably interesting classes of ship in the Norwegian Haugesund types, the Clyde-built Cardiff standard designs, and the Brazilian Prinasa 26s. The SSM ships were particularly familiar in Australian and New Zealand ports – Lyle in particular had carried cargoes for the British Phosphate Commissioners for many years, and the association carried over to the benefit of SSM.

• *Cape Ortegal* – Lyle Motorship Co (Scottish Ship Management), UK; Govan Shipbuilders, Glasgow, 1976; 26,931dwt, 175m, 5ha, 4 x 18tn cr, 11,600bhp Harland & Wolff-B&W. (Tolerton) • *Baron Pentland* – H Hogarth & Sons (Scottish Ship Management), UK; Govan Shipbuilders, Glasgow, 1976; 26,815dwt, 175m, 5ha, 4 x 18tn cr, 11,600bhp Harland & Wolff-B&W. (Tolerton) • *Cape Grafton* – Lyle Shipping Co (Scottish Ship Management), UK; Haugesund M/V A/S, Haugesund, 1971; 24,090dwt, 162m, 5ha, 4 x 16tn cr, 12,000bhp 2 x Stork-Werkspoor. (Tolerton)

From top, the Cardiff types *Cape Ortegal* and *Baron Pentland* and the Haugesund-built *Cape Grafton*. The Hogarth ship, with a rather more elaborate superstructure than the *Cape Ortegal*, was built in only 15 weeks at Govan. The *Cape Grafton* is pictured handling packaged lumber in Sydney and has SSM's original sea horse and trident funnel crest, while the other two have the much more mundane houseflag funnel emblem introduced in 1980.

Cape Horn – Lyle Motorship Co (Scottish Ship Management), UK; Haugesund M/V A/S, Haugesund, 1971; 24,035dwt, 162m, 5ha, 4 x 16tn cr, 12,000bhp 2 x Stork-Werkspoor. (Tolerton)

The twin funnels and tall superstructures of the Lyle's and Hogarth's Haugesund ships made them look rather larger than they were at 24,000dwt and 162m long. The bow view of the *Cape Horn* (above), arriving at a New Zealand port deeply laden with a phosphate cargo, exemplifies this. The *Cape Trafalgar* (below) was one of the four Brazilian-built Prinasa 26,000dwt bulkers that made up the last class of ships built for Scottish Ship Management. Completed in 1981, she was sold only three years later to become the Hong Kong-registered *Port Royal*, still managed by SSM.

Cape Trafalgar – Trafalgar Shipping Co (Scottish Ship Management), UK; CCN Maua, Niteroi, 1981; 26,060dwt, 173m, 5ha, 4 x 25tn cr, 13,300bhp Mecanica Pesada-MAN. (Tolerton)

Both Lyle and Hogarth made a huge investment in Norwegian-built bulkers, firstly with a group of seven 22,000dwt ships with six hatches and either four or three cranes, completed by Marinens Hovedverft, Horten, from 1968 to 1972. Ironically the Norwegian-built vessels largely competed with Norwegian-owned tonnage.

After the creation of SSM came orders for a series of ships from Haugesund Mekaniske Verksted – 15kn, self-trimming bulk carriers, 162m long and 24,000dwt, with five holds served by four 16tn cranes, and grab-fitted. Fuel consumption was about 36tn a day. Lyle received the *Cape Horn*, *Cape Hawke*, and *Cape Grafton* in 1971 and *Cape Grenville* in 1973, while Hogarth's vessels were the *Baron Ardrossan* of 1970, *Baron Inchcape* of 1971, and *Baron Wemyss* of 1972. Lambert's *Temple Inn* of 1972, managed by SSM, was another ship of this class. In 1979 the *Cape Hawke* had the distinction, appropriate for a Lyle ship, of taking the final phosphate cargo from Banaba (Ocean Island), destined for Australia.

Not even the keenest shipping enthusiast would say bulk carriers are beautiful, but the Haugesund ships, with their twin funnels, dramatic superstructures, and cranes set on tall pedestals, certainly looked majestic in SSM's pastel livery. Unfortunately for SSM, their machinery, twin medium-speed diesels from Ruston & Hornsby was less impressive. Repeated breakdowns forced the owners to replace the machinery – necessarily with twin medium-speed diesels again to fit the engineroom contours – in a huge and expensive programme in Amsterdam which took each ship out of service for about six weeks in 1973-1974. The Haugesund ships were refitted with twin Stork-Werkspoor engines driving a controllable pitch propeller (the *Grenville* had received this machinery before completion, when the problems with her sisters had already become apparent).

In comparison the four Cardiff class ships from Govan Shipbuilders were to be trouble-free, although ordering them must have given the two owners some misgivings. Both had been burned contracting with Govan's predecessor Upper Clyde Shipbuilders before this company went into liquidation in 1971.

The Cardiffs (the class was so named because the first orders were for Welsh owner Reardon Smith Line) were *Cape Ortegal*, *Cape Rodney*, *Baron Napier*, and *Baron Pentland*, all completed in 1976, and among 31 similar vessels completed to this design from 1970 to 1981.

Deadweight was 26,900 tonnes and overall length 175m, and the ships had 11,600bhp Burmeister & Wain engines from Harland & Wolff. Like the Haugesund ships, the Cardiff quartet were five-hatch vessels, with four 18tn cranes with electro-hydraulic grabs. Speed was again 15kn and fuel consumption 34tn a day.

The *Baron Pentland*, launched on April 29, 1976, took only 15 weeks to build from her keel-laying to launching.

SSM's last foray into new building was with four Prinasa PRI-26/15 standard 26,000dwt bulk carriers (originally ordered by Lloyd Brasileiro) from Cia Comercio e Navegacao of Rio de Janeiro. Bought for about US$62million, the *Cape Arnhem*, *Cape Trafalgar*, and *Baron Kinnaird* (1981) and *Cape Finisterre* (1982) were 173m long, five-hold ships with four 25tn Liebherr cranes with electro-hydraulic grabs. Shipbuilders were now offering provision for containers as an extra in some bulk carrier designs, and the Prinasa design could accommodate 648 TEUs in the holds and on deck. The ships were fitted with 13,300bhp MAN engines driving them at 15kn, and fuel consumption was 34.5tn a day.

In 1982 three of the cranes of the *Baron Kinnaird* were damaged and left hanging over the side when she encountered severe weather after leaving Napier, New Zealand. However, SSM was encountering storms not only at sea. The 1980s were grim for bulk carrier operators, and the new Brazilian quartet could not turn around SSM's fortunes at a time of depressed freight rates. Flagging out the ships to Bermuda in 1984, with Hamilton replacing Glasgow (Lyle) and, particularly regrettably, Ardrossan (Hogarth), on the sterns only delayed the inevitable.

In 1980 Lyle acquired Hogarth's 50 per cent share holding in SSM, and the next year Lyle was reported to be seeking to raise six million pounds capital. But the company, which had been publicly-listed since 1953 and could trace a history in shipping through almost two centuries, went into receivership in May, 1987. The last "Cape" sailing was by one of SSM's orphan vessels, the Mitsui-built Hong Kong-registered *Cape Otway* (1976/32,505dwt) which left Lyttelton, New Zealand, on December 1, 1987, for Brisbane, Australia and a change of name to *Hansa Mariner*.

Three of the Brazilian bulk carriers made news in August 1988 when they were auctioned in Darwin, Australia, on behalf of the Northern Territory Supreme Court. The *Kalapati* (ex-*Cape Trafalgar*), *Acacia I* (ex-*Cape Arnhem*), and *Adelfa* (ex-*Cape Finisterre*) had been laid-up at the port after being arrested in November 1987. They sold for US$24.05 million – or, as the Australian media noted, the price of 12,432,000 "tubes of Fosters."

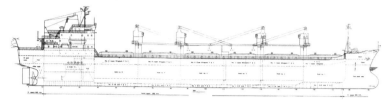

DIMENSIONS

LENGTH OVER ALL	= 522'-7 1/2"	=	159.293 m
BREADTH MOULDED	= 495'-0"	=	150.875 m
DEPTH MOULDED	= 75'-0"	=	22.860 m
DRAFT ON SUMMER FR.B.	= 42'-11"	=	13.080 m
DW. ON THIS DRAFT	= 21950 TONS		
GROSS TONNAGE	= 13436.59 TONS		
NET TONNAGE	= 7820.27 TONS		

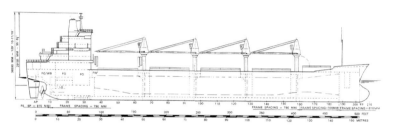

DIMENSIONS

LENGTH OVER ALL	= 534'-4"	=	162.86 m
LENGTH BETWEEN PP	= 505'-0"	=	153.90 m
BREADTH MOULDED	= 75'-0"	=	22.85 m
DEPTH MOULDED	= 46'-1 1/8"	=	14.05 m
DRAFT LOADED "S"	= 34'-1 1/8"	=	10.399 m
DEADWEIGHT ON THIS DRAFT	= 23655 TONS		
DISPLACEMENT EMPTY VESSEL	= 6395 TONS		

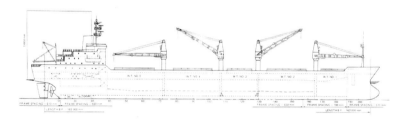

DIMENSIONS

LENGTH OVER ALL	=	173.159 m
LENGTH BETWEEN PP	=	162.000 m
BREADTH MOULDED	=	26.000 m
DEPTH MOULDED	=	13.500 m
DRAFT LOADED "S"	=	9.750 m
DEADWEIGHT ON THIS DRAFT	=	26066 TONS
DISPLACEMENT EMPTY VESSEL	=	7449 TONS

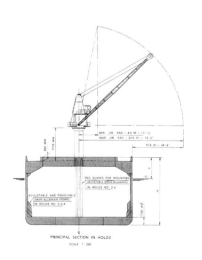

Profiles of three SSM classes – from top, the *Baron Maclay* and *Cape Leeuwin* from Horten, the twin-funnel *Cape Horn* Haugesund class, and the Brazilian-built *Cape Arnhem* types. At left, a hull cross-section of the Haugesund design, and the *Cape Otway* (1976/32,505dwt), chartered to the Australian National Line since 1981, making the last "Cape" sailing, leaving Lyttelton on December 1, 1987, for Brisbane where she was renamed. Her funnel was red with a black top instead of the SSM colours.

CHAPTER FIVE

BRITISH TRAMP COMPANIES

Scottish Ship Management's difficulties were mirrored by other tramp companies. Sir William Reardon Smith & Sons of Cardiff – its ships retained its founder's home town of Bideford as their port of registry – was another to make the transition to bulk carriers and build up a significant fleet, only to also fall victim to the sustained depression in this market. Reardon Smith's first bulk carriers were the 30,483dwt *Australian City* (1964) and *Eastern City* (1965) from Fairfield Shipbuilding and Engineering, followed by the 46,545dwt *Atlantic City* and similar *Indian City*, each costing about two million pounds, from the same yard in 1967.

The success of these ships encouraged further commitment by Reardon Smith and they and Upper Clyde Shipbuilders (Govan) liaised in the development of the Cardiff class 26,000dwt bulk carrier, Reardon Smith ordering the first four – the *Vancouver City*, *Prince Rupert City*, *Victoria City*, and *Fresno City*, and taking seven in all, while Irish Shipping, with which it participated in the Celtic Bulk Carriers pool (created in 1973), took four. As the names of the early completions suggest, the ships frequently carried forestry products from British Columbia, and were designed to be particularly suitable for this as well as general bulk.

Apart from the SSM quartet described earlier which had four cranes, the Cardiffs were equipped with five 15tn cranes, and as well as going to British and Irish owners were ordered by Danish, Hong Kong, Philippine, and London Greek owners. Like the SD14s, the Cardiffs had a distinctive ribbed appearance to their accommodation houses which made them readily identifiable. Reardon Smith – most of its ships now registered prosaically in Singapore instead of Bideford – went into liquidation in 1985.

The long-established Newcastle owner Chapman & Willan had three bulk carriers of particular interest before its exit from shipping. Two of these, the *Carlton* of 1964 and *Demeterton* of 1967, were to the Universal Bulk Ship design developed by MacGregor & Co, the prominent hatch cover and cargo-handling gear manufacturers.

The 20,448 dwt *Carlton*, the last and largest ship completed by Short Bros, Sunderland, was the first UBS built in Britain. The self-trimming UBS design incorporated a mix of top and main holds – four and five respectively in the case of the *Carlton*, with each of the upper holds divided transversely into three compartments, meaning 17 cargo spaces in total. The intention was to allow a vessel to carry her deadweight of most dry bulk cargoes (particularly grains) without excessive metacentric height and without shifting boards, but although both the *Carlton* and *Demeterton* gave various owners long service, the UBS did not prove the way of the future for dry bulk shipping.

Chapman & Willan's other bulk carrier, the *Frumenton* (1968/25,133dwt), was an early Japanese-built addition to the British register. She was launched by Hakodate Dock Co in 1968 as the *East Breeze* for Hong Kong's John Manners & Co, but sold to Chapman & Willan before completion.

Victoria City – Reardon Smith Line (Sir William Reardon Smith & Sons), UK; Upper Clyde Shipbuilders, Clydebank, 1970; 26,289dwt, 173m, 5ha, 5 x 15tn cr, 11,600bhp Kincaid-B&W. (APN)

The *Victoria City* of 1970 (above) was the third of seven Cardiff class 26,000dwt bulk carriers from Upper Clyde Shipbuilders delivered to Reardon Smith. Versatile five hatch bulkers, they were strengthened for ore cargoes and the decks for timber. The ship was sold in 1983 to become the *Lacandon* but remained under Reardon Smith management.

A minimal bridge was a feature of the *Sigsilver* (below), the largest pure bulk carrier in the world when completed for the Silver Line in 1967. The ship spent 13 years in Australian waters from 1973 on charter to Broken Hill Proprietary as the *Iron Sirius*.

Sigsilver – Silver Line, UK; Ishikawajima-Harima, Aioi, 1967; 107,476dwt, 250m, 11ha, 23,000bhp IHI-Sulzer. (World Ship Society)

• *Sugar Importer* – Albion Co (Sugar Line), UK; Caledon, Dundee, 1959; 16,160dwt, 170m, 6ha, 6 x 10tn der, 5500bhp Doxford. (Tolerton) • *Frumenton* – Carlton SS Co (Chapman & Willan), UK; Hakodate Dock, Hakodate, 1968; 28,169dwt, 181m, 7ha, 1 x 10tn cr, 12 x 10, 2 x 3tn der, 9600bhp IHI-Sulzer. (Tolerton) • *Temple Arch* – Euxine Shipping Co (Scottish Ship Management), UK; Horten Verft, Horten, 1969; 22,300dwt, 160m, 6ha, 3 x 10tn cr, 10,000bhp 2 x Ruston. (Tolerton) • *Stonepool* – Ropner Shipping Co (Ropner Management), UK; C Connell, Glasgow, 1966; 45,749dwt, 218m, 7ha, 13,000bhp Barclay, Curle-Sulzer. (World Ship Society)

Four early bulk carriers built for British tramp companies – from top, the Sugar Line's *Sugar Importer* of 1959, Chapman & Willan's *Frumenton* of 1968, Euxine Shipping Co's *Temple Arch* of 1969, and Ropner Shipping Co's *Stonepool* of 1966.

Other northeastern tramp companies that experimented with bulk carriers before disappearing from the shipping scene included the Stag Line (mentioned earlier), Stephens, Sutton, and Turnbull Scott. Turnbull Scott Shipping Co had three very large bulkers, but its experiences typified the difficulties for British companies making a transition from traditional tramp ships.

In 1966 the company took delivery from Furness Shipbuilding of the 72,030dwt *Naess Parkgate*, built against a 20-year bareboat charter to Anglo-Norness Shipping and utilising the low interest rates the British government was offering UK owners for domestic new building. She made her maiden voyage to Tubarao to load iron ore for Emden, then ballasted to the US Gulf to load grain at Pascagoula for European ports. The charter gave secure earnings to Turnbull Scott but did not provide the hands-on experience in managing a vessel of this size that the company would have liked.

The ship, renamed *Iron Parkgate* in 1973 when Australian mineral giant Broken Hill Proprietary chartered her, had an ill-starred life, dogged by mechanical and structural problems, and culminating in a fire at a Singapore dockyard in 1974 which killed 14 people.

Two years later Turnbull Scott took delivery of an even larger ship, the Swedish-built ore-oil carrier *Flowergate* (see Combination Carriers chapter) against a 10-year time charter. Both ships were sold in 1978, while a 71,705dwt newbuilding from Ishikawajima-Harima in 1974 was sold on delivery to a Rethymnis & Kulukundis company.

One of the significant British bulk carrier fleets for almost three decades was that of Tate & Lyle's Sugar Line of London. The company made a contribution to the development of bulk shipping when it put the war-built Empire Malta-class ships *Sugar Transporter* and *Sugar Refiner* into service at the start of the 1950s carrying raw sugar in bulk to the UK. These raised quarter deck, engines-aft collier-type vessels proved extremely suitable, and set in motion the development of specialised fleet of bulk carriers for the Sugar Line. Trading was by no means confined to carrying raw sugar to the UK – they also operated as ore and grain carriers, and appeared as far afield as New Zealand (the *Sugar Importer* in 1972).

In 1979 the Sugar Line finished when the fleet, then composed of two 29,000dwt ships only five-years-old and four smaller and slightly older ships was sold.

Two of the giants of world grain trading – traditionally dominated, like oil, by a small group of majors – operated British flag bulk carriers through UK subsidiaries.

Buries Markes, a subsidiary of French grain giant Louis Dreyfus & Co, had a reputation for innovative ships, and its fleet evolved from conventional tramps to bulk carriers via vessels like the 14,500dwt *La Loma* of 1959, an engines-aft tween-decker designed to carry both bulk cargoes and, utilising portable decks, vehicles. The French-built *La Chacra* (1963/24,664dwt) was the company's first true bulk carrier, and a steam ore-oil carrier, the 249,223dwt *La Loma* of 1972, had the distinction of being the largest vessel Buries Markes owned. As a Dreyfus company, Buries Markes also contributed ships to the highly successful Gearbulk group, which is covered later in the chapter on open hatch bulk carriers.

Trader Navigation Co, also London-based, was another British shipping arm of a major grain trader, in its case Brazil-based Bunge & Co. The *Scottish Trader* of 1962, *Middlesex Trader* (1963), *Surrey Trader* (1964), and *Essex Trader* (1968) were all Austin & Pickersgill completions which introduced bulk carriers to the Trader Navigation fleet before Bunge decided to abandon ship-owning in 1971.

Offsetting the famous names that have disappeared, some British companies have navigated successfully into this century, although not necessarily through total reliance on bulk carriers.

The Silver Line was one name that did not vanish completely. Over the years this company operated in both liner and tramp shipping and the oil trades, and built its first ore carriers in the late 1950s. In 1963 it, too, experimented with car/bulk carrying. The *Totem Star* and *Totem Queen*, renamed *Silverbeach* and *Silversea*, initially operated carrying cars from Germany to North America and grain back from the Great Lakes, and later a five month round-trip schedule of British cars to the United States, American grain to Japan, Japanese cars to the US Gulf, and American grain to Britain and Europe. Thus laden every time they sailed, they must have been fine earners for Silver Line.

Oakworth – Watergate Steam Shipping Co (R S Dalgleish), UK; Cammell Laird, Birkenhead, 1972; 33,880dwt, 180m, 7ha, 4 x 10tn cr, 15,000bhp Doxford. (APN)

The 33,880dwt *Oakworth*, one of a trio of sisters along with one slightly smaller ship built by Cammell Laird for prominent Newcastle owner R S Dalgleish, is launched at Birkenhead in 1972. When the conventional tramps had had their day, many tramp owners like Dalgleish made a natural transition to bulk carriers. Its first was the *Silksworth* of 1964. The company went into liquidation after selling the *Oakworth* (renamed *Progressist*) and her sisters to mainland China's Hong Kong shipping company Ocean Tramping in 1978-1979.

The company was among the first to order from Japan with the 18,656dwt *Silvercove* of 1967 from Namura Zosensho and the 107,476dwt *Sigsilver* from IHI the same year. The latter, the largest bulk carrier at the time, was renamed *Chelsea Bridge* in 1971 for Seabridge service. She became the *Iron Sirius* in 1973 on charter to BHP, carrying iron ore out of Port Hedland from the newly-developed Mt Newman mine in Western Australia to Newcastle and Port Kembla. The ship had 11 holds and, like some contemporary tankers, an extremely narrow bridge front with stub wings to minimise windage. BHP operated her until 1986, by which time she'd carried 10.8 million tonnes of ore and 500,000 tonnes of coal for this company.

Silver Line continued to think big, contributing seven more ships of more than 100,000dwt to Seabridge. Taken over by the Vlasov group in the 1973, it managed combination carriers and bulk carriers as well as other vessels for Vlasov, like the 225,898dwt ore-oil carrier *Alva Bay* of 1973, one of two British-flagged sisters from Gotaverken. After operating in the oil trades in the 1970s, the ship was time-chartered to carry iron ore from Tubarao to Rotterdam for Krupp steelworks. Sold after 10 years, she was scrapped only three years later.

Vlasov's V Ships started the new century as the world's largest ship management company with about 600 under its wing in 2002, and the group preserved the Silver Line name for its commercial division. It also lingers incongruously in the names of the cruise liners of Silversea, which the Lefebvre family, who'd been involved in Sitmar Cruises, started in the 1990s.

Representative of Silver's dry bulk operations, here is its fleet positions/cargoes, late 1976:

Erskine Bridge Coal, Hampton Roads to Japan, there to drydock.
Progreso Argentino Petcoke to Japan.
Puerto Acevedo Japan to South America.
Puerto Madryn South American coastal trading.
Puerto Rocca Coal, Hampton Roads to Argentina; grain from River Plate.
Severn Bridge Sold to American buyers, November.
Silverclyde Voyage charter for BHP, Australia to Antwerp (carrying sheep on deck Fremantle-Jeddah).
Silvercove Sugar, Queensland to St John, New Brunswick.
Silverdon Timecharter Star Shipping, Pacific Basin trading.
Silverfjord Timecharter NYK, cars Japan to Jeddah.
Silverforth British Steel pipes, Newport to Kandla.
Silvermain HBS pool, cars Nagoya to Houston.
Silvertweed Drydocked Yokohama October, then sugar, Australia to east coast USA.
Stirling Bridge Time charter, iron ore, Australia to Europe.
Avon Bridge (OBO) Sold to American buyers, December.
Docebay (ore/oil) Iron ore, Brazil to Japan, and oil, Arabian Gulf to Brazil.
Silver Bridge (OBO) Iron ore, Brazil to Japan, there to drydock.

Graig Shipping, still headquartered in historic Bute St, Cardiff is also active today in ship-owning and other maritime services after successfully weathering the storms of bulk carrier operation and diversifying. Started in 1919 by Idwal Williams, this fleet was never one of the largest tramp concerns, but has flourished when many much larger companies have disappeared. The first Graig bulk carrier was the 28,825dwt *Graigwerdd* of 1964 from Scotts, and the company bought and sold adroitly to operate a small fleet into the 1990s. The largest were the 108,649dwt *Graigffion* (ex-*Skaufast* of 1968) and 108,148dwt *Graiglas* (ex-*Alnwick Castle* of 1973), both bought in 1983.

Graig is set to make its mark in the new century with a series of double-hull 53,000dwt bulkers to the Diamond 53 design which it jointly developed. Ships to this design are on order for Graig and other operators from both Chinese and Vietnamese shipyards.

"Ropner's Navy" was once the largest tramp fleet, and it survives as Ropner Ship Management – now based in Kent instead of the north-east. Its bulker involvement started early with the 17,170dwt *Wandby* from Bartram & Sons in 1959. She was a very successful ship which remained in Ropner's fleet until 1972, by which time she was dwarfed by the likes of the 108,503dwt Harland & Wolff sisters *Rudby* and *Iron Somersby* of 1971, both ordered after Ropner had joined four

Norwegian companies in the Norwegian Bulk Carriers consortium. *Iron Somersby* was chartered on completion by BHP, becoming the first Australian-operated 100,000-tonner. Although her career was initially disrupted by industrial disputes, the ship carried 13,788,000 tonnes of iron ore and coal in 136 voyages for BHP before redelivery to Ropner at the end of 1986.

Ropner went even bigger with two more vessels from Harland & Wolff, the 119,500dwt *Lackenby* in 1977 and 117,613dwt *Appleby* in 1978, both chartered to British Steel.

Although prominent Glasgow company J & J Denholm directly owned few bulk carriers itself, its long involvement in ship management brought a large fleet of bulkers and other vessels under its wing. Its management operations started in the 1950s, when Denholm was the leading operator of the small ore carriers built for BISC service. Denholm developed its management expertise through its association with the enterprising Norwegian-American owner Erling Naess, and was a model of flexible evolution in British shipping in an era when so many similar owners went to the wall. Denholm Ship Management was merged into Hong Kong's Anglo-Eastern Ship Management in 2001, the marriage of east and west creating the world's fifth largest ship manager looking after more than 200 ships.

The 33,190dwt *Mountpark* of 1965 from Charles Connell was in the Denholm fleet nine years, and the *Glenpark* (1971/27,480dwt) from Upper Clyde Shipbuilders, Scotstoun, a seven-hold vessel with five 8tn cranes, had a 12 year career with Denholm. In April 1982 the ship loaded what was reported as New Zealand's largest export bulk grain cargo, 23,000 tonnes of barley from Timaru for Saudi Arabia. The *Wellpark* (1977/29,554dwt) from Mitsubishi Heavy Industries, Hiroshima, was Britain's last cadetship, accommodating 24 deck officer cadets, and had five holds served by one 25tn and three 15tn cranes, and four derricks. She was renamed *Ga Chau* in 1984, and operated under Denholm management for another 10 years before being sold as the *Nava Avra*. In 2004 she was still in service as the Chinese *Firstec*.

The *Glenpark* had also been briefly renamed *Ga Chau* and registered in Hong Kong in 1982, then sold as the *Halla Caravan* in 1983 after Denholm had taken delivery in 1982 of the 30,670dwt standard design *Broompark* – Denholm's 100th ship, and seventh ship of this name – from Sunderland Shipbuilders, Pallion. Built at a cost of 9.5 million pounds (the first of the name in 1910 cost 16,900 pounds), the *Broompark* had five 15tn cranes serving six holds, and went into service in the Atlantic Bulkers pool. Unusually for a handysize bulk carrier, she did not have a bulbous bow. She was originally registered in Glasgow, this changing to Douglas two years or so later. She was sold in 1999, becoming the *Millenium Raptor*.

Atlantic Bulkers was formed by Denholm, Sweden's Brostrom group, and James Elwell of New York (which operated Liberian-flag ships) in 1969, and later Bowring, Blue Funnel, T & J Harrison and its Hong Kong associate Blairdale Shipping, and two Singapore owners were also members.

Some representative voyages of Denholm's bulkers:

Glenpark Discharged Uddevalla, ballast to the St Lawrence. Grain, Three Rivers to Hsinkang. To Vancouver, sulphur to Tauranga and Napier. To Adelaide, bagged barley, to Gizan and Jeddah. To New Haven, shredded scrap to Bombay. Ballast to Sydney, coal to Kanda. To Nauru, phosphate for New Zealand.

Wellpark Sugar, Mourilyan to Baltimore. Grain, Baltimore to Whampoa. Bunkers, Hong Kong, To Queensland. Sugar, Mourilyan and Cairns to Philadelphia. Ballast to Mississippi. Phosphate, Taft to Navlakhi. To Durban for drydocking. Maize, Durban to Kaohsiung. To Christmas Island. Phosphate to Lyttelton, Bluff, and Nelson. Coal, Brisbane to Kanda. To Nauru. Phosphate, to Lyttelton, Timaru, Bluff, and Dunedin. Grain, Brisbane to Singapore.

Glenpark – Denholm Line Steamers (Denholm Ship Management), UK; Upper Clyde Shipbuilders, Scotstoun, 1971; 27,480dwt, 176m, 7ha, 5 x 8tn cr, 2 x 3tn der, 11,600bhp Kincaid-B&W. (Tolerton)

Wellpark – Denholm Line Steamers (Denholm Ship Management), UK; Mitsubishi, Hiroshima, 1977; 29,554dwt, 170m, 5ha, 1 x 25, 3 x 15tn cr, 12,000bhp Mitsubishi-Sulzer. (Tolerton)

Broompark – Denholm Line Steamers (Denholm Ship Management), UK; Sunderland Shipbuilders, Pallion, 1982; 30,670dwt, 188m, 6ha, 5 x 15tn cr, 12,000bhp Clark Hawthorn-Sulzer. (Tolerton)

Denholm have managed dozens of bulk carriers, but the Glasgow company's owned fleet was small. From top, the *Glenpark* of 1971, cadetship *Wellpark* of 1977, and *Broompark* of 1982

Bowring Steamship Co of London was another historic company which after operating in a notable variety of shipping spheres finally bowed out of the industry with bulk carriers. In its latter days the Bowring fleet included three handysizes including the *Trinculo* (left) and three Panamaxs like the *Sydney Bridge* (below) which operated in the Seabridge pool.

Trinculo – Bowring SS Co, UK; Swan Hunter Shipbuilders, Hebburn, 1978; 28,972dwt, 182m, 5ha, 4 x 15tn cr, 12,000bhp Barclay, Curle-Sulzer. (Tolerton)

Sydney Bridge – Bowring Steamship Co, UK; Harland & Wolff, Belfast, 1970; 59,662dwt, 224m, 7ha, 15,900bhp Harland & Wolff-B&W. (APN)

Cairnsmore – Detiga Shipping Co (Indo-China Steam Navigation Co), Hong Kong; Austin & Pickersgill, Sunderland, 1982; 34,800dwt, 182m, 5ha, 4 x 25tn cr, 10,400bhp Clark Hawthorn-Sulzer. (Tolerton)

Austin & Pickersgill, Sunderland, offered several handysize standard designs, and the *Cairnsmore* of 1982 (above) for Jardine Matheson was the first B35 type – only seven years after a previous *Cairnsmore* had been the first of A&P's 26,000dwt B26 series. Registered in Hong Kong, the bow emblem and the thistle crest on the bridge front paid tribute to the hong's Scottish heritage. Jardine Matheson has had a deft touch for joint shipping ventures, and although shipping is just one of the group's activities it still prospers in it through IndoChina Ship Management, in partnership with Pacific Basin group. The 1982 *Cairnsmore* was sold to Greek owners as the *Captain Sarantis* after only four years.

Britannia – Verney Services Corp (Wallem Ltd), UK; Sanoyas Hishino Meisho, Kurashiki, 2001; 48,377dwt, 187m, 5ha, 4 x 30tn cr, 10,699bhp Diesel United-Sulzer. (Tolerton)

The red ensign continues to fly at the stern of bulk carriers in the 21st century, even if the British fleet is much reduced from 20 years ago. A notable addition, if only for her name, in 2001 was the London-registered *Britannia* (above), a 48,377dwt standard design from Sanoyas Hishino Meisho – and launched at the Mizushima shipyard to the strains of "God Save The Queen" by a Japanese brass band. Commissioned by Ocean Bulk Carriers of London, the ship was put in Wallem management. There have been no reports of Her Majesty holidaying aboard. An earlier version of this Sanoyas design was the *San Paolo* (below). This ship and her sister *San Pietro*, both of 1995, were also British ships, registered in Douglas and managed by Scinicariello Ship Management of Naples. Like the *Britannia*, they are five-hold vessels with four 30tn cranes.

San Paolo – Azara Shipping (Scinicariello Ship Management SpA), Isle of Man (UK); 46,601dwt, 187m, 5ha, 4 x 30tn cr, 9133bhp Diesel United-Sulzer. (Tolerton)

14 M

8

6

4

2

13 M

8

6

4

2

12 M

8

6

4

2

11 M

8

6

4

2

10 M

8

6

4

2

9 M

8

6

4

2

8 M

8

6

4

2

7 M

8

6

4

2

6 M

8

6

4

CHAPTER SIX

EX-BRITISH SHIPS

Chanda – Mackinnon Mackenzie & Co, India; Marinens Hovedverft, Horten, 1968; 22,333dwt, 160m, 6ha, 4 x 8tn cr, 9600bhp Horten-Sulzer. (Tolerton)

Yes, that is a British India funnel on this Indian bulk carrier. Lyle's *Cape Wrath* of 1968 was sold to Mackinnon Mackenzie & Co of Bombay in 1976 to become the *Chanda*, a name that had been used for three BI ships. The owners, their name redolent of BI's founders and former Indian managing agents, also adopted another familiar BI name, *Teesta*, for a second bulk carrier (formerly the *Tokai Maru* and also acquired in 1976) that they operated. The *Chanda* had to be towed to Falmouth in 1978 after machinery failure on a voyage from the Great Lakes to Rotterdam, but then served her Indian owners until she was laid up in Bombay in 1988. She went to local breakers in 1991.

Freeport – Kingsnorth Shipping Co (Valiant Shipping Co, London), Greece; Burmeister & Wain, Copenhagen, 1973; 51,891dwt, 218m, 7ha, 4cr, 13,100bhp B&W. (Tolerton)

The Anchor Line's Burmeister & Wain standard design *Cameronia* of 1973 was sold four years later to Anders Jahre to become the Norwegian flag *Jalanta* and converted for vehicle carrying. She was resold in 1982 to the Vergottis-owned London-based Valiant Shipping Co. Originally a gearless bulker, she was subsequently fitted with four cranes.

Katerina – Katerina Navigation Co (DST Shipping), Malta; G Dimitrov, Varna, 1983; 25,570dwt, 185m, 7ha, 4 x 16tn cr, 12,000bhp Cegielski-Sulzer. (Kevin Moore)

The small London company Hadley Shipping Co (associated with Houlder Bros) survived in tramp shipping much longer than many of the bigger and more famous operators. One of its later vessels was the Bulgarian standard type *Corato* which after completion in 1983 was modified for an eight month UK Ministry of Defence charter as a transshipment storage vessel at the Falklands, where the extra accommodation of an East European ship proved invaluable for the MOD personnel. Bermuda-flagged, she was sold in 1994, and is pictured as the Maltese *Katerina*, her fifth name.

Orgullo – Orgullo Navigation (Allied Maritime, Athens), Panama; Austin & Pickersgill, Sunderland, 1976; 26,600dwt, 183m, 7ha, 14 x 10tn der, 9900bhp Clark-Sulzer. (Kevin Moore)

The former Houlder Brothers *Upwey Grange*, a 26,600dwt standard B26 design from Austin & Pickersgill in 1976 and sold six years later, was sailing under her sixth name as the Panamanian *Orgullo*. It was also the name she carried when she arrived at Alang in 2002 for breaking up.

Kilmun – Stanhope Shipping (Eastern Bulkers), Hong Kong; Govan Shipbuilders, Glasgow, 1976; 26,931dwt, 175m, 5ha, 4 x 18tn cr, 11,600bhp Harland & Wolff B&W. (Tolerton)

Showing the distinctive lines of the Govan-built Cardiff types, the *Kilmun* was Lyle Shipping's *Cape Ortegal* until 1982. She was one of several Scottish Ship Management bulkers transferred to the management of Eastern Bulkers, Hong Kong, and given "Kil" names, the Scottish names and a livery similar to SSM's suggesting the sale did not totally severe the connection with their original owners. The *Kilmun*, owned by Stanhope Shipping when she was managed by Eastern, within a year or two returned to SSM management under the ownership of Swiftbright Co, before she was sold again to the Philippines in 1986 as the *Esperanza V*. She had at least four more names before she was scrapped.

CHAPTER SEVEN

SPECIALISED TYPES:
1 THE GIANTS

Economies of scale became quickly apparently in dry bulk shipping, as in the oil trades. Growth in the size of ships was rapid from the late 1960s, and today a number of bulk carriers of more than 300,000dwt are employed.

An early milestone came in 1967 with the completion of the British *Sigsilver* by Ishikawajima-Harima, Aioi, for the Silver Line. With a deadweight of 94,944 later revised to 107,476dwt, she was the largest pure bulk carrier in the world. The following year Harland & Wolff, Belfast, completed the 108,649dwt *Skaufast* for Norwegian owner I M Skaugen as the largest bulk carrier built in Europe. The 260m, nine hatch vessel was built to carry iron ore for a Dutch steel company, and was followed by a sister *Aino* from Harland & Wolff for another Norwegian owner, Sorensen & Sonner. In 1982 the Wah Kwong ore carrier *Hitachi Venture* provided a new yardstick for size at 267,889dwt and 324m long.

They are left far behind by today's largest bulk carrier, the 364,767dwt ore carrier *Berge Stahl* (below), which has had that distinction since completion by Hyundai Heavy Industries at Ulsan in 1986. She is 343m long with a beam of 63.5m and maximum draught of 23m. The ship went into service with a 10-year charter to carry iron ore from Brazil to Rotterdam for shipment on to German steel works – and could move 4 million tonnes a year

Originally Liberian-flagged but later transferred to the Norwegian register, the monarch of the world's bulkers, with a service speed of 13.5kn, consumes 71tn of fuel a day.

Berge Stahl – P/R Berge Stahl ANS (Bergesen dy A/S), Norway; Hyundai, Ulsan, 1986; 364,767dwt, 343m, 10ha, 24,858bhp Hyundai-B&W. (Bergesen)

Berge Atlantic – P/R Bergesen GOIC DA (Bergesen dy ASA), Norway; Hyundai, Ulsan, 1998; 171,882dwt, 291m, 9ha, 26,740bhp Hyundai-B&W. (Bergesen)

Another Bergesen giant is the *Berge Atlantic*, a 1998 171,882dwt completion from Hyundai. Believed to be the largest double-hull bulk carrier when she went into service and the first from the world's biggest shipbuilder Hyundai, the *Berge Atlantic* has nine holds, flush deck, and a speed of 16kn. She was built to carry iron ore to the UK on a British Steel charter.

Onga Maru – NYK Line, Japan; IHI, Kure, 1985; 198,906dwt, 300m, 8ha, 15,655bhp IHI-Sulzer. (Markus Berger collection)

Major Japanese companies like NYK and Mitsui OSK operate many of the largest bulk and ore carriers to satisfy the insatiable demand of Japan's iron and steel works. One of the more innovative giant bulkers was NYK's ore carrier *Onga Maru* which went into service in 1985 carrying iron ore from West Australia for Nippon Steel. She had four holds and eight hatches. A feature was an air resistance-reducing vane on either side of the superstructure. Designers predicted the vanes would have a rectifying effect in head winds and act like a sail to assist propulsion in side and tail winds, contributing to fuel saving. This ship also had a new bulbous open stern also intended to assist fuel economy.

8

4

2

14 M

8

6

4

2

13 M

8

6

4

2

12 M

8

6

4

2

11 M

8

6

4

2

10 M

8

6

4

2

9 M

8

6

4

2

8 M

8

6

4

2

7 M

8

6

4

2

6 M

8

6

4

CHAPTER EIGHT

SPECIALISED TYPES: 2 CONBULKERS

Conbulkers represent an attempt to operate in two spheres, container and bulk, with the one ship. The failure of the two most serious ventures in this field, Cast and ABC Containerline, suggest that rather than being a jack of all trades, it is better to be master of one, and in 2004 when 600 container ships were on order for delivery to 2006, only four were conbulkers.

Cast operated conbulkers like the Hyundai-built *Cast Otter* (1982/70,870dwt), one of a trio of 14.5kn vessels carrying up to 1466 TEUs, in its North Atlantic service. Carrying bulk cargoes like ore from St Lawrence River ports to north Europe eastbound and containers back, they also had accommodation for 12 passengers. Cast was also active in OBOs, operating the largest fleet in the world at one time. Cast's parent, Eurocanadian Shipholdings, went into receivership in 1983, but restructuring enabled the trans-Atlantic service to continue.

Even more ambitious was the round the world service of Tsvi Rosenfeld's Belgian-based ABC Containerline (the initials standing for Antwerp Bulk Carriers), which linked Europe, Australia, New Zealand, the US Gulf, and the US east coast, undercutting the conference lines on the service "down under." ABC collapsed in 1996. While Cast and ABC gave established container lines a run for their money for a number of years, the relatively slow speed of the conbulker was a handicap for a container line service.

A more successful conbulker story appears to be that of the open hatch-type *Thuleland* (below), built by Eriksbergs as one of two sisters for Sweden's Brostrom group in 1977. Able to carry 832 containers in her holds and on deck, the 15kn ship has five 25tn cranes serving six holds. Fuel consumption is 49tn a day, and she has a bow thruster. More than a quarter of a century after completion, the *Thuleland* is still trading under her original name – and in 2004, after operating under the Swedish and Singaporean flags, was under the British flag – appropriately owned by Veteran Shipping Ltd!

Thuleland – Cranston Pte Ltd (ASP Shipmanagement Singapore Pte), Singapore; Eriksbergs, Gothenburg, 1977; 31,900dwt, 185m, 6ha, 5 x 25tn cr, 15,140bhp Eriksbergs-B&W. (Kevin Moore)

Ellen Hudig – Maritime Carriers Luxembourg SA (ABC Containerline NV), Luxembourg; Boelwerf, Hoboken, 1983; 42,077dwt, 209m, 9h, 16,800bhp Cockerill-Sambre-Sulzer. (Tolerton)

The ultimate conbulker? *Ellen Hudig* with the *Cornelis Verolme* made up ABC's third (and last) generation of conbulkers. The Luxembourg-flagged vessel had a speed of about 18kn and carried 1111 containers, 666 in her nine holds and 445 on deck. Up to 610 containers were refrigerated. Sold in 1997 to become the Cypriot *Hellen C* (below), she still has the orange ABC funnel and remnants of the ABC emblem. Since 2003 she has operated for Mediterranean Shipping Co, that twilight home for so many old container ships, as the *MSC Gianna*.

Hellen C – Lorain Shipping Co (Cyprus Sealines SA), Cyprus. (Kevin Moore)

4

2

14 M

8

6

4

2

13 M

8

6

4

2

12 M

8

6

4

2

11 M

8

6

4

2

10 M

8

6

4

2

9 M

8

6

4

2

8 M

8

6

4

2

7 M

8

6

4

2

6 M

8

6

4

CHAPTER NINE

SPECIALISED TYPES: 3 COMBINATION CARRIERS

Ship owners, by nature a thrifty breed, have the frustration of knowing that if they operate tankers or dry bulk carriers, their ships are on non-earning ballast passages much of their time at sea. Ore-oil and OBO (ore-bulk-oil) carriers have attempted to address that.

A far cry from the enormous and sophisticated combination carriers to come later were two pioneer ore-oil carriers, Swedish owner Grangesberg-Oxelosund's 12,100dwt *Rautas* of 1945 and *Raunala* of 1946 from Gotaverken. The Norwegian 23,870dwt *Bomi Hills* from Fairfield Shipbuilding in 1952 was the first of the considerably larger ore-oil carriers of the 1950s, carrying iron ore in their self-trimming centre compartments on one leg of their voyages and oil in the side tanks on the other. These led to the OBO as a further refinement.

The OBO, whose development owed much to Norwegian entrepreneur Erling Naess, had the advantage of being able to carry either oil or dry bulk cargoes in its holds, secured by gas-tight hatches. Ore cargoes are carried in alternate holds. The Weser-built, Liberian flag 71,183dwt motorship *Naess Norseman* of 1965 was the first OBO classed by Lloyd's and had 11 holds. Another notable early OBO was the Liberian flag *San Juan Trader* of 1966 from Nippon Kokan, a 63,410dwt ship built to carry ore from Peru to Japan, Europe, and the USA, and coal, oil, or other bulk cargoes on the returns. Both ore-oil carriers and OBOs – particularly the former – grew rapidly in size and by the 1970s combination carriers of more than 200,000dwt were in service.

Lloyd's Register records the world fleet of combination carriers growing from 8.317 million gross tons and 207 ships in 1970 to 26.241 million gt and 424 ships in 1980 and 19.769 million gt and 360 ships in 1990. By 2000 it had dropped to 8.615 million gt and 205 ships.

The combination carrier minimized ballast voyages and theoretically gave operators flexibility to capitalize on the ups and downs of either the dry bulk or oil markets, albeit at the price of a higher initial investment than for a similar-sized pure tanker or bulker. By the 1990s orders for

combination carriers tapered off. Ship owners, it seems, see the future lying with dedicated tankers or dry bulk carriers. The flawed safety record of combination carriers has probably been a factor in this decline, and this is looked at later in this book.

In 1970 the OBO *Hoegh Rainbow* became the largest dry cargo vessel to discharge at a UK port when she arrived at Port Talbot with iron ore. *Hoegh Rainbow* – PR Hoegh Rainbow (Leif Hoegh & Co AS), Norway; Kawasaki, Kobe, 1970; 101,193dwt, 250m, 7ha, 20,700bhp Kawasaki-MAN. (APN)

Probo Gull – Probo Gull Inc (Torvald Klaveness & Co), Norway; Korea Shipbuilding, Pusan, 1989; 47,980wt, 182m, 7ha, 2 x 28tn cr, 12,788bhp Hyundai-B&W. (Tolerton)

Norway's Klaveness group has always been prominent in this sector, and the Norwegian-flag *Probo Gull* of 1989 (above) was one of a notably versatile class of six Panamax-beam 48,000dwt OBOs for it. Also suitable for product carrying as the "Probo" prefix signaled and with special provision for caustic soda cargoes, this ship from Korea Shipbuilding has seven holds/tanks with pontoon hatch covers, two 28tn traveling cranes, a container capacity of 954 TEUs, inert gas system and crude oil washing, coated holds, and a double-hull. Conspicuous is the free-fall lifeboat. The *Probo Gull* and a sister were sold for US$42 million to a United Arab Emirates company set up in 1996, in which Klaveness was a partner. A recent Panamax size OBO for Klaveness, Oslo-registered like the *Probo Gull*, is the *Banasol* (below). One of four sisters, this 72,700dwt ship from Oshima Shipbuilding has seven holds and two small cranes for cargo residuals.

Banasol – Banasol Inc (Torvald Klaveness & Co), Norway; Oshima, Oshima, 2001; 72,700dwt, 225m, 7ha, 11,864bhp Kawasaki-B&W. (Tolerton)

Flowergate – Turnbull Scott Shipping Co, UK; Gotaverken, Gothenburg, 1968; 106,700dwt, 253m, 8ha, 14 wing tk, 19,200bhp Gotaverken. (Turnbull Scott)

A giant in the fleet of well-known British tramp operator Turnbull Scott was the ore-oil carrier *Flowergate* of 1968 (above), from Gotaverken, which was a leader in the construction of combination carriers. Turnbull Scott took over the building contract from Grangesberg against a 10-year time charter back to the Swedish company. The ship had an unpromising start to her career – major engine faults required four months of repairs at Rotterdam after her first round voyage. With four holds and 14 wing tanks, the 106,700dwt ship initially operated for two years carrying iron ore from West Africa to Japan, then ballast to the Arabian Gulf to load crude oil for Europe-United Kingdom. The *Flowergate* was then sub-chartered to a Gulf Oil subsidiary for 18 months carrying crude oil from the gulf to both Far East and European ports.

Another Swedish-built British combination carrier was the London-registered *Scandia Team* (below), a 105,550dwt, nine-hold ore-oil carrier from Oresundsvarvet which Denholm managed. Some representative voyages: Oil, Dumai-Long Beach/Port Angeles, then ballast to San Nicolas, then ore, San Nicolas-Pohang. Ore, Monrovia-Rotterdam. Coal, Hampton Roads-Dunkirk. Dry dock, Singapore, then iron ore, Cape Lambert-Redcar.

Scandia Team – Team-Ship VI Ltd (Denholm Ship Management), UK; Oresundsvarvet, Landskrona, 1974; 103,929dwt, 256m, 9ha, 19,800bhp Gotaverken. (Markus Berger)

SKS Tana – SKS Obo Holding (V Ships Norway AS), Norway; Hyundai, Ulsan, 1996; 109,906dwt, 243m, 7ha, 1 x 15tn cr, 19,100hp Hyundai-B&W (C Lous)

The *SKS Tana* of 1996 was the first of a series of 10 innovative Aframax-size OBOs from Hyundai for SKS Obo of Bermuda, designed to overcome the operational shortcomings of earlier combination carriers. Built with pure epoxy-coated cargo tanks, these ships are double-hulled and constructed with a much reduced use of high-tensile steel to minimise corrosion and hull fatigue problems. Each of the seven holds/tanks has a hydraulic deepwell pump to avoid dry cargo residue contaminating oil cargo valves. SKS Obo is a joint venture of major Norwegian dry bulk operator Kristian Jebsen and Chile's Compania Sud Americana de Vapores.

The state of the art *SKS Tana* makes an interesting contrast with the British-flag steam turbine *Mobil Energy* (below), a 72,771dwt OBO with six holds. Built by Eriksbergs at Gothenburg in 1962 as one of four conventional tankers for Mobil, she was rebuilt as an OBO nine years later by Mitsubishi, Kobe, with a new forward section of six holds/tanks.

Mobil Energy – Mobil Shipping Co, UK; Mitsubishi, Kobe, 1971 (aft, Eriksbergs 1962); 72,771dwt, 252m, 10ha, 18,000shp 2 x Laval steam turb. (Markus Berger collection)

6

4

2

14 M

8

6

4

2

13 M

8

6

4

2

12 M

8

6

4

2

11 M

8

6

4

2

10 M

8

6

4

2

9 M

8

6

4

2

8 M

8

6

4

2

7 M

8

6

4

2

6 M

8

6

4

CHAPTER TEN

SPECIALISED TYPES: 4 OPEN HATCH BULK CARRIERS

Among the most sophisticated bulk carriers are the open hatch, gantry crane ships – a segment of the market dominated by a handful of companies.

The pioneers of this type were the Norwegian 9200dwt six-hold ships *Besseggen* and *Rondeggen* of 1963, built by Kaldnes and designed to carry newsprint on the North American west coast. Looking for an improvement on slowly loading rolls by rope slings and laboriously stowing them in the holds of conventional ships, naval architect Robert Herbert of the Seattle firm Philip F Spaulding designed the first open hatch ship.

The holds were giant open boxes occupying most of the width of the ship, with hydraulically-operated MacGregor folding hatch covers that were the largest in the world at the time. The three Munck travelling gantry cranes were equally innovative, and fitted with special spreaders to handle eight rolls at a time.

The success of the Kaldnes vessels in their specialised trade led to the much larger open hatch bulk carriers that have followed – carrying not only newsprint, but other unitised cargoes as diverse as packaged lumber, wood pulp, plywood, steel coils, aluminium ingots, and containers as well as conventional dry bulk commodities, and often on a liner service. However, it's a tribute to Herbert's original design that the basic concept of these ships is little-changed today. Preeminent among the companies operating these vessels are Gearbulk, with more than a third of the tonnage, and Star Shipping, with a similar share.

Gearbulk started in 1968 as a joint venture of Louis Dreyfus of Paris, its British subsidiary Buries Markes of London, and two Norwegian companies J Ludwig Mowinckels and Kristian Gerhard Jebsen, both of Bergen – all companies already established in the bulk trades. Jardine Matheson was involved as manager of a number of the ships. In 1991 Jebsen bought out the holdings of its partners, and the Japanese giant Mitsui OSK also became involved in Gearbulk, taking a 40 per cent holding.

The Gearbulk fleet – the ships generally operated under the flag of Bahamas – has been upgraded regularly through orders placed in groups at a variety of shipyards (Japan, Korea, China, and Poland) over three decades, and the vessels have increased in size to 51,500dwt. However, the typical appearance of a Gearbulk open hatch ship has not changed, with two dominating travelling gantry cranes with their hydraulically-operated cantilever extensions for discharging cargo from the box holds, pontoon hatch covers, and the pronounced knuckle either side near the bow to allow the foremost crane to serve No.1 hold.

Most Gearbulk cargo is carried under contracts of affreightment and it is adept at avoiding ballast voyages. Gearbulk has its own terminals around the world to support its services.

Bergen-based Star Shipping was created in 1962 and owned by Norwegian companies Westfal-Larsen, Fred Olsen, and A/S Billabong. As well as managing its large fleet of open hatch vessels, Star Shipping has been a prominent operator of geared handysize bulk carriers with chartered vessels, and in 2004 was operating 40 open hatch vessels and 30 geared handymaxs. Like Gearbulk, it has set up a number of its own terminals.

Star Shipping has also regularly upgraded its fleet, and the *Star Herdla* and *Star Hidra* of 1994 from Mitsui were the first of eight 45,000dwt 16kn "eighth generation" open hatch ships, each with two 40tn gantry cranes, from Mitsui and Daewoo.

A new class from Stocznia Szczecinska starting with the *Star Ikebana* of 1999 brought a new look for the open hatch type, being flushdeckers with a large breakwater near the bows. In addition five of the nine main holds have cell guides and a small 10th hold has 20 reefer plugs.

Grena – K/S Arrow Bulk VIII (J Ludwig Mowinckels), Norway; Nipponkai, Toyama, 1974; 38,635dwt, 182m, 5ha, 2 x 25tn gantry cr, 13,100bhp Mitsui-B&W. (Tolerton)

A typical earlier Gearbulk open hatch vessel – the *Grena*, renamed *Hato Arrow* in 1991, was a 1974 Japanese-built contribution to the group from Mowinckels. Prominent are the two 25tn gantry cranes, and the ship could carry up to 1100 TEUs.

Global Explorer – Ba Than Maritime, Myanmar; Shin Kurushima, Onishi, 1996; 24,800dwt, 153m, 4ha, 4 x 30tn cr, 8400bhp Mitsubishi. (Tolerton)

The 24,800dwt Myanmar-flag *Global Explorer*, completed in 1996 by Shin Kurushima for major Japanese operator Daiichi Chuo Kisen, is a new design of open hatch ship with four 30tn conventional cranes. She's designed to carry all timber and lumber cargoes, chips, and other bulk cargoes, and the box holds and raised freeboard give a greater capacity than ordinary log carriers. The sunken deck aft is a distinctive feature of this design.

6

4

2

14 M

8

6

4

2

13 M

8

6

4

2

12 M

8

6

4

2

11 M

8

6

4

2

10 M

8

6

4

2

9 M

8

6

4

2

8 M

8

6

4

2

7 M

8

6

4

2

6 M

8

6

4

CHAPTER ELEVEN

SPECIALISED TYPES: 5 SELF-DISCHARGING BULK CARRIERS

Self-unloading bulk carriers developed on the Great Lakes, and the 27,230dwt Canadian steamship *Cape Breton Miner* of 1964 for John D Leitch of Toronto was a pioneer self-unloader designed to operate both on the Great Lakes and, when the St Lawrence Seaway closed in winter, as an ocean trader. Nowadays self-unloaders are a small but interesting segment of the world's bulk carrier fleet, with vessels ranging from quite small bulkers (an area which Kristian Jebsen seems to have dominated with its partners in this sector, Thunbolaget of Sweden and Aboitiz of the Philippines) to vessels of up to Panamax size and greater. Canadian Steamship Lines, which introduced its first self-unloader in 1924, and Egon Oldendorff have been leaders operating the larger ships.

Oldendorff has operated two of the largest self-dischargers, the 77,500dwt *Yeoman Burn* and *Yeoman Brook*, both completed in 1991 by Daewoo Shipbuilding, Okpo, for 20 year charters to Foster Yeoman, a British minerals and quarries company. Discharge from the hoppered holds is via conveyor belts to a 76m long swivel boom. An even bigger self-unloader was the 105,708dwt *Sage Sagittarius* from Imabari in 2001, the first of a trio built to service a new Japanese coal terminal, and able to discharge 2000tn an hour through an automated, computer-controlled system incorporating two gantry cranes each with a 50tn grab, and a hopper-conveyor system.

A typical self-discharging bulk carrier is the *Express* of 1990 (below) of Australia's Howard Smith Industries, which took the name of the founder's first ship. Built by Tsuneishi Zosen and registered in Hobart, the 17,309dwt ship could discharge up to 2500 tonnes an hour, and showed her versatility by carrying sulphate of ammonia, gypsum, and wheat in her initial voyages. Discharge from her four holds is remote controlled from the bridge, cargo feeding through 32 gates at the bottom of the holds onto a conveyor belt and to the unloading boom at the bow. Designed to handle virtually any bulk cargo, the *Express* has holds coated with a Teflon-type material for cargo to slip easily to the conveyor belt, and both bow and stern thrusters. However, her career with Howard Smith was relatively short. She was sold to a Jebsen company as the *Trimnes* in 1996 when Howard Smith withdrew from ship-owning.

Express – Howard Smith Industries Pty, Australia; Tsuneishi, Numakuma, 1990; 17,309dwt, 149m, 4ha, 5755bhp Akasaka-Mitsubishi. (Tolerton)

River Torrens – Australian National Line, Australia; NSW State Dockyard, Newcastle, 1977; 31,921dwt, 181m, 5ha; 11,600bhp Hitachi-B&W. (Tolerton)

Two Australian self-discharging bulk carriers, both of which have had rather chequered careers, in the colours of the Australian National Line: The *River Torrens* (above) and *River Yarra* (below). Built in Australia in 1977 as a conventional gearless bulk carrier for ANL's domestic trading as the *Selwyn Range*, the *River Torrens* was converted in 1985 to become the first self-unloader on the Australian coast. She and the *River Yarra*, which had been completed in 1984 as the *Star Kanda* by Kanda Zosensho, were sold to a Canada Steamship Lines subsidiary in 1999 – and both sailed into industrial troubles over flag issues. The latter, now renamed *CSL Yarra*, was described as "turning into a nice big concrete block" by CSL in 2002 after a fire hose was opened into a hold containing 700tn of cement, and CSL incurred union wrath operating the *River Torrens*, now renamed *CSL Pacific*, registered in Bahamas and with a Ukrainian crew, on the Australian coast.

River Yarra – ASP Ship Management, Australia; Kanda, Kawajiri, 1984; 32,452dwt, 182m, 4ha, 11,200bhp Hitachi-B&W. (Tolerton)

4

2

14 M

8

6

4

2

13 M

8

6

4

2

12 M

8

6

4

2

11 M

8

6

4

2

10 M

8

6

4

2

9 M

8

6

4

2

8 M

8

6

4

2

7 M

8

6

4

2

6 M

8

6

4

CHAPTER TWELVE

SPECIALISED TYPES: 6 WOOD CHIP CARRIERS

The demands of Japan's paper manufacturing industry led to the development of one of the most specialised and distinctive bulk carrier types, the wood chip carrier. Like most bulk carrier types, its story has been one of fine-tuning rather than dramatic design innovations as the type evolved. Wood chips are a very low density cargo, hence the characteristic high-sided appearance of these ships.

The first chip carrier was the *Kure Maru* of 1964, built by Nippon Kokan for Nippon Yusen Kaisha against cargo guarantees from Toyo Pulp Co. The ship had five holds and an air trimmer on either side of the deck to convey the chips into the hold, using compressed air, as they came down the conveyor.

On modern wood chip carriers – the largest can carry more than 4million cubic feet of chips – cargo can be discharged at nearly 1000 tonnes an hour. Ships are fitted with high speed cranes with "orange peel" grabs, and conspicuous hoppers on deck. The chips are unloaded into these hoppers and carried forward via conveyor belts to be discharged from doors at the bow.

Most of the chip carrier fleet operates for major Japanese companies like NYK and Mitsui OSK, and like ore carriers are built against cargo guarantees. North American, New Zealand, and Australian forestry provides the cargoes.

As in other areas of shipping, vessels have grown steadily in size. Sanoyas Hishino Meisho built a series of 44,000dwt woodchip carriers to Panamax beam in the 90s, and the 209m, 53,793dwt *Dynastar* (37m beam) from the same builder in 1997 was probably the first "overpanamax" chip carrier.

Pictured below is a large early chip carrier, the *Taikai Maru* of 1971, a 28,848dwt ship operating for the Mitsui OSK subsidiary Nihonkai Kisen. Chip ships do not have the large discrepancy between gross and deadweight tonnage of ordinary bulk carriers, and the gross tonnage figure of the *Taikai Maru*, 31,951, was in fact greater than the deadweight.

Taikai Maru – Nihonkai Kisen KK, Japan; Sumitomo, Yokosuka, 1971; 28,848dwt, 196m, 6ha, 3 x 10tn cr, 11,200bhp Sumitomo-Sulzer. (Tolerton)

Honshu Silvia – Honshu Maritima SA (NYK Line), Panama; Imabari, Marugame, 1989; 35,166dwt, 179m, 6ha, 3 x 12tn cr, 7700bhp Akasaka-Mitsubishi. (Tolerton)

As in so many areas of bulk shipping, NYK is to the fore in wood chip carriers. Typical of its fleet is the Panamanian *Honshu Silvia* of 1989 (above), a 35,166dwt six-hatch vessel with three 12.5tn cranes and four hoppers which are prominent in this photograph of her loading at Port Chalmers, New Zealand. The mountain of wood chips ready to be loaded is to be seen at right. The *Keoyang Majesty* of 1997 (below), also Panamanian-flag, is one of two six-hatch sisters built by Hanjin for the Hanjin group company Keoyang Shipping. She has three 17tn cranes and four hoppers.

Keoyang Majesty – GOA Leasing International (Keoyang Shipping Co), Panama; Hanjin, Pusan, 1997; 48,618dwt, 221m, 6ha, 3 x 17tn cr, 13,206hp Hanjung-B&W. (C Lous)

4

2

14 M

8

6

4

2

13 M

8

6

4

2

12 M

8

6

4

2

11 M

8

6

4

2

10 M

8

6

4

2

9 M

8

6

4

2

8 M

8

6

4

2

7 M

8

6

4

2

6 M

8

6

4

CHAPTER THIRTEEN

SPECIALISED TYPES: 7 LOGGERS

It is hard to look past the humble logger if you're looking for the vessel most representative of Far East shipping. These robust ships (until recent years generally of less than 30,000dwt) with their characteristic stanchions evolved as specialised bulk carriers to replace the conventional tramp ships and converted lumber carriers in this trade, although they are capable of handling other bulk cargoes, too.

Their loading ports range from the river mouths and creeks of the East to dedicated facilities in log-exporting countries like New Zealand, where a log stacking area is a feature of most ports and the loading a streamlined procedure.

A major early group of specialised log ships was ordered by Nippon Yusen Kaisha starting with the *Matsue Maru* of 1964. All with names starting with "matsu" (pine), the five were 15,700dwt ships built to carry lumber from North America and New Zealand, and the last was completed in 1966.

In recent years the logger has become a target for environmentalists. It is estimated that illegal timber may make up more than a tenth of the world timber trade – and, it is claimed, more than half of the logging in some areas like South East Asia and the Amazon basin. This has been a particular concern for Indonesia, but actions to combat it like its seizure of three loggers in November 2001 and two more in January 2002 have had limited success.

Away from the shady end of the trade, companies like Japan's Inui Steamship Co (a Mitsui OSK subsidiary and one of the first companies to operate specialist log ships) and South Korea's Pan Ocean Shipping Co are leaders in this sphere of bulk shipping. However, while eastern operators dominate it, European companies like Delmas-Vieljeux, Leif Hoegh, and Deutsche Afrika (all in the West African trade), and East Asiatic Co have also had significant involvement in log shipping.

The logger, like most bulk carrier types, may seem to have changed little outwardly, but in fleets like Inui and Pan Ocean small but subtle changes in their new tonnage over the years have marked the evolution of the logship.

Left: The mate's view of loading on a logger using the ship's cranes. Work has finished at some hatches and the logs on deck secured by strong wire lashings (photo, Martin Woodhall).

Sarinderjit – Blue River Navigation Pte, Singapore; Kochiken, Kochi, 1975; 10,145dwt, 127m, 3ha, 4 x 20tn der, 6000bhp Kobe-Mitsubishi. (Tolerton)

The classic eastern logger: The 10,145dwt *Sarinderjit* was completed by Kochiken Zosen in 1975 as the *Ocean Explotar* and three years later became the *Extraco II*, before becoming the *Sarinderjit* in 1990 as part of the small fleet of Singapore's Tradeco Enterprises. She has three hatches and four 20tn derricks on two pole masts.

Iran Fallahi – Islamic Rep. Of Iran Shipping Lines, Iran; Kasado, Kudamatsu, 1972; 33,657dwt, 185m, 5ha, 5 x 22tn der, 11,550bhp Sumitomo-Sulzer. (Tolerton)

Another 1970s logger was the *Iran Fallahi*, built by Kasado Dock Co in 1972 as the Liberian-flag *Eastern Lilac* for Hong Kong's World-Wide Shipping and acquired by Islamic Republic of Iran Shipping Lines in 1984. A much larger ship at 33,657dwt, she had five holds and five 22tn derricks mounted high on goalpost masts.

Sun Harvest – Aoba Kosan KK (Usui Kaiun KK), Japan; Koyo, Mihara, 1978; 18,801dwt, 147m, 4ha, 4 x 25tn der, 7800bhp IHI-Pielstick. (Tolerton)

Logships have made up a large portion of the output of Japan's smaller shipyards, like the 18,801dwt *Sun Harvest* of 1978 from Koyo Dockyard. She had four hatches and four 25tn derricks. In spite of her flag of convenience name, she was Japanese-flag, and also unusual in being registered at the relatively small small port of Sendai, capital of Miyagi prefecture, rather than one of the major ports. Built as the *Seiriki*, she changed name in 1980.

Dooyang Winner – Dooyang Line Co, South Korea; Imabari, Marugame, 1986; 40,016dwt, 189m, 5ha, 4 x 30tn cr, 6929bhp Hitachi-B&W. (Tolerton)

South Korea, like Japan, is a major log importer, and the *Dooyang Winner* of 1986 was part of the Dooyang Line fleet, established in 1984 through several almalgamations but much reduced after Dooyang filed for bankruptcy protection in 1998. Her cargo is secured by both fixed (lighter colour) and collapsible stanchions as she completes loading. By now cranes were the norm for log ships, and this vessel, one of a group of very large loggers built by Imabari Zosen, has four 30tn cranes serving five hatches.

Emerald Bulker – Botelho Shipping Corp (Fairmont Shipping Canada Ltd), Philippines; NKK, Tsu, 1995; 28,255dwt, 166m, 5ha, 4 x 30tn cr; 6711bhp Mitsui-B&W. (Tolerton)

A laden logship under way invariably makes a striking picture, as the two loggers on this page show. The *Emerald Bulker* (above), a typical modern logger, is a 28,255dwt Philippine-flag 1995 completion from NKK Corporation (formerly Nippon Kokan). The four 30tn cranes, enclosed lifeboat, and satcom dome are contrasts to the earlier loggers illustrated. Fuel consumption for the 14kn ship is 21tn a day. One of a 26,000dwt series from Usuki Tekkosho, the *Moonlight Success* of 1986 (below) is another Philippine-flag vessel and part of the huge fleet of bulk carriers of all sizes trading for Mitsui OSK, the biggest operator of all in dry bulk shipping. Built as the *Sun Orchid*, the ship had had six changes of name by the end of 1994 when she had become the *Moonlight Success* for the second time. This view of her under way illustrates why log ship cranes are on tall pedestals to work the cargo.

Moonlight Success-- Manila Transworld Carriers (Shinwa Marine Corp, Tokyo), Philippines; Usuki, Saiki, 1986; 26,849dwt, 174m, 5ha, 4 x 30tn cr, 7170bhp Mitsubishi. (Tolerton)

4

2

14 M

8

6

4

2

13 M

8

6

4

2

12 M

8

6

4

2

11 M

8

6

4

2

10 M

8

6

4

2

9 M

8

6

4

2

8 M

8

6

4

2

7 M

8

6

4

2

6 M

8

6

4

CHAPTER FOURTEEN

WESTERN EUROPEAN-BUILT BULK CARRIERS

Bulk carrier construction is a sphere of shipbuilding that Western Europe's remaining yards have almost entirely relinquished, but Western European yards held their own until Japan and then South Korea forged ahead of them from the 1970s.

The 15,667dwt *Sally Stove* of 1961, below, was an early French-built bulk carrier for Lorentzens Rederi, one of many Norwegian companies to have been prominent in dry bulk shipping. Completed by Ch. Reunis Loire-Normandie, it may go too far to say she has a touch of French elegance, but this photograph certainly shows how much even bulkers have changed in 40 years. The 14.75kn ship had seven hatches served by 14 5tn derricks, and was sold in 1970 to become the *Nortrans Gloria*.

Pictured (over page, top) in the distinctive funnel colours of Greek owner Fafalios, the 24,973dwt *Mairoula* was a 1963 Belgian delivery from J Boel & Fils, Tamise, built as the *Irene S Lemos* and sold to fellow Greek owners in 1973. Although completed only two years after the *Sally Stove*, her owners opted for six 5tn cranes to serve her six hatches, but two 5tn stores derricks are conspicuous aft.

German shipyards were prominent early in bulk carrier construction. The vessel pictured (over page, bottom) in the 1990s as the Chinese *Hua Fang*, was launched by Luebecker Flender-Werke in 1971 as the *Hermann Schulte* for Schulte & Bruns, taken over by another German owner in 1978 as the *Marianne Bolten,* then sold to China in 1984. The tall goalpost masts are characteristic of many German vessels of her time, and she had 14 5tn derricks serving seven hatches. Speed was 16.5kn.

Sally Stove – Lorentzens Skibs (Lorentzens Rederi Co), Norway; Ch.Reunis Loire-Normandie, Nantes, 1961; 15,667dwt, 155m, 7ha, 14 x 5tn der, 6300bhp Ch. de l'Atlantique-Sulzer. (APN)

Mairoula – Compania Concordia de Navegacion SA Panama (Nea Tyhi Maritime Co), Greece; J Boel, Tamise, 1963; 24,973dwt, 183m, 7ha, 6 x 5tn cr & 2 x 5tn der, 10,500bhp MAN. (Tolerton)

Hua Fang – Shanghai Hai Xing Shipping Co, China; Luebecker Flender-Werke, Luebeck, 1971; 33,373dwt, 196m, 7ha, 14 x 5tn der, 13,500bhp Borsig-Fiat. (Tolerton)

Vaship – Wellington Shipping Co, Cyprus; Van der Giessen, Krimpen, 1970; 20,015dwt, 160m, 5ho (9ha), 5 x 8tn cr, 7500bhp Sulzer. (Tolerton)

The Nedlloyd group had a significant investment in bulk shipping with vessels like the one above, pictured as the Cypriot *Vaship* near the end of her career. Completed as the *Putten* in 1970 by Van der Giessen-de Noord, she became the *Amsteldiep* in 1977 and after disposal by Nedlloyd in 1985 traded as the *Novsun*, *Sailor II*, *Vaship*, *Mascot*, *Kokoni*, and *Rea Fotini*. She had five 8tn cranes serving five holds. Another bulker with a pedigree looking humble in her last years was the *Offi Gloria* (below), a 28,402dwt vessel from Cantieri Navali del Tirreno e Riuniti, Ancona. She was the first of two sisters Danish owner DFDS ordered from the Italian yard in an uncharacteristic excursion into bulk shipping in which DFDS's sister company J Lauritzen has been so prominent. However, after her launch as the *Unitrader* the yard took over the contract and delivered her in 1968 to Fratelli d'Amico as the *Mare Dorico*. She subsequently operated as the *Nereo*, *Elizas Grace*, *Beauty E*, and *Stardrop* before becoming the *Offi Gloria* for Cypriot owners in 1990. Strengthened for ore cargoes, she had seven holds and 14 8tn, two 5tn, and two 1tn derricks.

Offi Gloria – Prescott Shipping Co, Cyprus; Cant. Nav. del Tirreno & Riuniti, Ancona, 1968; 28,402dwt, 186m, 7ha, 14 x 8tn, 2 x 5tn, 2 x 1tn der, 10,500bhp B&W. (Tolerton)

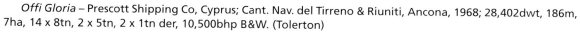

Valetta – Sameiet Valetta (Halfdan Ditlev-Simonsen & Co), Norway; Oresundsvarvet, Landskrona, 1968, 26,880dwt, 175m, 7ha, 2 x 10 & 3 x 8tn cr, 4 x 5 & 2 x 3tn der, 10,350bhp Gotaverken. (APN)

Swedish builders like Oresundsvarvet of Landskrona were to the fore in bulkship construction, often for Norwegian owners. The *Valetta* of 1968 for Ditlev-Simonsen of Oslo was a typical example. The 27,484dwt ship was built to the specifications of the British Phosphate Commissioners for long-term charter to them and is pictured (above) discharging at the New Zealand port of Timaru. Ditlev-Simonsen was among the major operators in the phosphate trade from Nauru, Christmas, and Ocean Islands. Were cranes or derricks more efficient? Her owners, like many in this era, had a bet both ways – the *Valetta* had five cranes and six derricks.

Ariadne – Nils W Svensson, Sweden; Gotaverken, Gothenburg, 1972; 103,332dwt, 256m, 9ha, 21,600bhp Gotaverken. (Berger collection)

Swedish shipyards built many combination carriers in the 1960s and 70s like the 103,332dwt *Ariadne* of 1972, a motor OBO from Gotaverken for Nils W Svensson of Gothenburg. She had nine holds and 14 tanks.

Vigsnes – Jebsen Thun Short Sea SA (Aboitiz Jebsen Bulk Transport Corp), Panama; Kleven, Ulsteinvik, 1979; 6105dwt, 107m, 3ha, 2 x 12tn cr, 4000bhp Werkspoor. (Tolerton)

A quite different Scandinavian bulker from the previous two was the *Vigsnes* of 1979 (above), built by Kleven, Norway, for Kristian Jebsen. Bergen-based Jebsen has always been notably enterprising in filling market niches and establishing joint ventures and partnerships, and the *Vigsnes*, a 6105dwt ship with three holds and two 12.5tn cranes, is typical of many smaller bulkers the company has operated. Aboitiz, a leading transport operator in the Philippines, has been a close partner of Jebsen for more than 20 years.

Nephele – Neptune Maritime Co of Monrovia (Poseidon Shipping Co), Greece; Verolme, Cork, 1983; 71,927dwt, 226m, 7ha, 15,906bhp 2 x Krupp-MaK. (Tolerton)

Built as the *Irish Spruce*, the 71,927dwt Livanos Panamax *Nephele* had the distinction of being the last and largest ship built for Irish Shipping, and also the largest ship built at the Verolme Cork Dockyards. When Irish Shipping went into liquidation at the end of 1984, this ship was arrested at Marseilles, and sold to become the *Eagle* in 1986 and then in 1987 the *Nephele*. Her machinery was unusual – two medium speed 6cy MaK engines, with fuel consumption of 44tn a day, instead of a conventional low speed diesel – and was intended to be more economical slow steaming on ballast passages and to offer maintenance advantages. She also had folding hatch covers rather than the side-rolling covers usual on Panamaxs.

Alexis – Dryden Maritime (Tomasos Brothers), Gibraltar; Astilleros Espanoles, Bilbao, 1984; 27,048dwt, 182m, 7ha, 4 x 10tn cr, 9500bhp AESA-Sulzer. (Kevin Moore)

Spanish state shipbuilder Astilleros Espanoles had great success with its handysize standard bulk carriers – the 21,000dwt Santa Fe (although this one primarily in a tweendecker version), the 27,000dwt Euskalduna, 30,000dwt Sevilla, and 35,000dwt Vizcaya designs. Production of the seven hatch Euskaldunas ran for 20 years from the late 1960s. One of the last completions was the Gibralter-registered *Alexis* (above), from Bilbao in 1984 as the *Ocean Crony*. Representative of the Vizcaya class is the Yugoslav *Bled* of 1983 (below) from the Seville yard. She had five holds served by four 16tn cranes and fuel consumption of 39tn a day.

Bled – Genshipping Corp (Splosna Plovba), Yugoslavia; Astilleros Espanoles, Seville, 1983; 34,947dwt, 197m, 10,900bhp AESA-B&W. (Tolerton)

4

2

14 M

8

6

4

2

13 M

8

6

4

2

12 M

8

6

4

2

11 M

8

6

4

2

10 M

8

6

4

2

9 M

8

6

4

2

8 M

8

6

4

2

7 M

8

6

4

2

6 M

8

6

4

CHAPTER FIFTEEN

B&W'S PANAMAXS

Probably no Panamax types are more immediately recognisable than former Copenhagen shipbuilder Burmeister & Wain's contributions in this size. And with more than 60 built over about 25 years before B&W's closure, this was the most successful West European Panamax. From the first 52,000dwt ships built in the early 1970s, the B&W Panamax evolved through to the 75,000dwt Mark Five vessels commencing with the *Romandie* of 1994 for Suisse-Atlantique SA. The more than 20,000 tonne increase in deadweight capacity was effected, along with various technical improvements, with only slight change to the basic hull dimensions, and the hull design was also the basis for B&W Panamax tankers.

It's perhaps a tribute to the design that British liner companies Anchor Line (with the *Cameronia* of 1973, *Caledonia* of 1975, and *Calabria* of 1977), T & J Harrison (*Specialist* and *Strategist* of 1976), Blue Funnel (*Helenus* and *Hector* of 1973), Canadian Pacific (*Port Vancouver* and *Port Quebec* of 1977), and P&O (with the geared 1983-built secondhand purchase *Malvern*, later renamed *Quorn*) were among the operators of these ships. A 1977 completion saw service with two more, built for China Navigation as the *Eredine* and sold to Ben Line in 1981 to become the *Benalbanach*. And two were delivered to Denmark's illustrious EAC in 1976, the *Morelia* and *Malacca*. They also found ready buyers with companies like COSCO which commissioned four of the 20 BC60E2 version ships completed from 1981 to 1985.

Below is the *Wen Zhou Hai* of 1982, still operating for COSCO more than 20 years after completion as the first of the quartet for the Chinese state owner.

Wen Zhou Hai – COSCO Bulk Carrier Co, China; B&W, Copenhagen, 1982; 64,170dwt, 225m, 7ha, 12,600bhp Mitsui-B&W. (Tolerton)

Beauforte – Turnville Shipping (Nippon Marine Service Co), Philippines; B&W, Copenhagen, 1981; 64,120dwt, 225m, 7ha, 12,600bhp Mitsui-B&W. (Tolerton)

The first BC60E2 was the *Danelock* of 1981, pictured above as the *Beauforte*, after her third change of name, and flying the ensign of the Philippines. She was one of six of this type, some of them geared, completed for the Wheelock Marden group of Hong Kong and sold after its collapse in 1985. The distinctive bow shape and the conspicuous frames supporting the hatch coamings are prominent in this photograph. Unlike the earlier B&W Panamaxs, the later Mark Four and Five versions of the 90s had a plumb bow – and the *Romandie* also introduced a Sulzer engine instead of B&W machinery. At least five of the design's final incarnation were built in Italy, like the *Luigi D'Amato*, below, completed in 1996 as one of two for Fratelli D'Amato of Naples by Fincantieri. Fuel consumption of 32 tonnes a day for her 5cy Sulzer engine compares with 40 tonnes for the *Wen Zhou Hai*.

Luigi D'Amato – Fratelli D'Amato SpA, Italy; Fincantieri-Cant. Nav. Italiani, Venice, 1996; 75,300dwt, 225m, 7ha, 13,051bhp Fincantieri-Sulzer. (Tolerton)

4

2

14 M

8

6

4

2

13 M

8

6

4

2

12 M

8

6

4

2

11 M

8

6

4

2

10 M

8

6

4

2

9 M

8

6

4

2

8 M

8

6

4

2

7 M

8

6

4

2

6 M

8

6

4

CHAPTER SIXTEEN

EASTERN EUROPEAN-BUILT BULK CARRIERS

Poland, with the deepest seafaring tradition of the Slavic countries, has been at the forefront of both shipping and shipbuilding in Eastern Europe since World War Two. With coal and shipbuilding Poland's major export industries, bulk carriers have featured significantly in both the domestic fleet and in construction at its shipyards.

The gearless 32,000dwt B447 design from Stocznia Szczecinska has been one of the most successful designs. More than 20 were built in the early and mid 1970s, half of them for the Polish Steamship Co (PZM), the state tramping, bulk, and tanker company, like the *Cedynia* (1973/ 31,910dwt), pictured below speeding to destruction – exiting Durban in November 2001 on her way to the Alang shipbreakers.

The B517-type from the same builder was the later version – also a nine-hatch vessel of similar dimensions to the B447. Pictured (overleaf, top) is PZM's *Uniwersytet Slaski* (1979/33,470dwt).

The B547-types like the *Kopalnia Rydultowy* (1990/11,702dwt), overleaf, centre, were a class of smaller geared bulk carriers from Szczecinska. She is fitted with five cranes, four of them 16tn and paired and one 12.5tn. All three are of course ice-strengthened.

Polish yards received many orders from the Soviet Union. As well as building three B470 types for PZM, Stocznia im Komuny Paryskiej at Gdynia built seven for the USSR, like the *Zorinsk* (1970/ 22,687dwt) pictured overleaf, bottom.

Cedynia – SMS Lib Ltd (Polish Steamship Co), Panama; Stocznia Szczecinska, Szczecin, 1973; 31,910dwt, 199m, 9ha, 12,000bhp Cegielski-Sulzer. (Kevin Moore)

Uniwersytet Slaski – Polish Shipping Co, Poland; Stocznia Szczecinska, Szczecin, 1979; 33,470dwt, 198m, 9ha, 12,000bhp Cegielski-Sulzer. (Marcelo Lopes)

Kopalnia Rydultowy – Polish Steamship Co, Poland; Stocznia Szczecinska, Szczecin, 1990; 11,702dwt, 143m, 5ha, 1 x 12tn & 4 x 16tn cr, 5182bhp Cegielski-B&W. (Marcelo Lopes)

Zorinsk – Black Sea Shipping Co, USSR; Stocznia im "Komuny Paryskiej," Gdynia, 1970; 22,687dwt, 187m, 7ha, 9600bhp Cegielski-Sulzer. (Tolerton)

Pine Arrow – Erica Maritime SA (Kristian Gerhard Jebsen Skipsrederi A/S), Bahamas; Stocznia Gdanska, Gdansk, 1996; 48,041dwt, 190m, 7ha, 4 x 36tn cr, 12,100bhp Cegielski-B&W. (Tolerton)

More sophisticated bulk carriers from Poland have included vessels for the Gearbulk open-hatch fleet – both ships with gantry cranes and with conventional cranes, like the 48,041dwt Bahamas-flag *Pine Arrow*, designed for forest products and also equipped to carry 1556 containers in her seven holds and on deck. She's also fitted with bow thruster.

South Cross – South Cross Shipping (Seastar Maritime Management, Piraeus), Panama; Varna Shipyard JSC, Varna, 1994; 40,926dwt, 186m, 5ha, 4 x 30tn cr, 11,336bhp Bryansk-B&W. (Tolerton)

Like Poland, Bulgaria developed its shipbuilding industry almost from scratch after World War Two, and series construction of bulk carriers has been a major part of its output. The 40,926dwt *South Cross* was completed in 1994 at Varna Shipyard as the *Captain Nicholas* and can carry 1102 containers in her five holds and on deck. She also traded as *Captain Nicholas I* and *Sea Orchid* before becoming the *South Cross* in 2003.

Graigwerdd – Graig Shipping (Idwal Williams & Co), Bermuda; Georgi Dimitrov, Varna, 1982; 38,095dwt, 201m, 7ha, 5 cr, 15,000bhp Bryansk-B&W. (Tolerton)

Welsh owner Graig Shipping's 38,095dwt *Graigwerdd*, above, was one of a long series of standard ships when Bulgaria was part of the Soviet bloc and the Varna yard was the Georgi Dimitrov Shipyard. Built as the *Vari*, she was bought by Graig in 1987 and registered in Hamilton, Bermuda. The yard's other specialty was a 24,000dwt bulker, built in both geared and gearless versions, like the British Cayman Islands-flagged *Christy* of 1983 (below). She was completed as a gearless vessel, the *Akademik Davitaya*, for the Soviet Union's Georgian Shipping Co, and had four 16tn cranes fitted later in her career.

Christy – Christy Shipping (Eurocarriers SA), Cayman Islands; G Dimitrov, Varna, 1983; 24,150dwt, 181m, 7ha, 4 x 16tn cr, 12,000bhp Cegielski-Sulzer. (Kevin Moore)

Mount Ymitos – Astrolabe Shipping (Kassos Maritime Enterprises, Athens), Malta; Santierul Naval 2 Mai, Mangalia, 1983; 54,158dwt, 220m, 10ha, 17,400bhp UCM Resita-MAN. (Tolerton)

Romania was an even later comer to building oceangoing ships, and is another East European country active in bulker construction. The Maltese-flag *Mount Ymitos* of 54,158dwt was a seven-hold, 10-hatch gearless bulker from Santierul Naval 2 Mai Mangalia, launched as the *Christina*, but renamed *Bailesti* and operated by Romanian state owner Navrom until her sale in 1992. Representative of handysize construction from the same yard is the 29,089dwt *Svitava* of 1995, operating for Czech Ocean Shipping of Prague under the Maltese flag (below). She was launched as the *City of Sunderland*.

Svitava – COS-Star (Czech Ocean Shipping Joint-Stock Co, Prague), Malta; Santierul Naval 2 Mai, Mangalia, 1995; 29,089dwt, 180m, 5ha, 4 cr, 8198bhp Bryansk-B&W. (Tolerton)

Lok Sahayak – Mogul Line, India; Santierul Naval, Galatz, 1975; 18,003dwt, 145m, 4ha, 8 cr, 7200bhp Cegielski-Sulzer. (Tolerton)

One of five smaller Romanian bulkers built for India's Mogul Line by Santierul Naval Galatz was the *Lok Sahayak*, above. Her departure to Alang shipbreakers early in 1986 suggests a career not without mishap. Both the Soviet Union and the new Russia have made limited contributions to the world's oceangoing bulk carrier fleet. An example of modern Russian construction is the *Georgia T* (below), which was launched in 1998 by Baltiyskiy Zavod, St. Petersburg, as the *Transworld 3* but not put into service until 2002. She has four 35tn cranes.

Georgia T – Sea Strength Marine (Modion Maritime Management SA, Piraeus) Malta; JSC Baltiyskiy Zavod, St Petersburg, 2002; 48,640dwt, 190m (bp), 5ha, 4 x 35tn cr, 14,139bhp Sulzer. (Tolerton)

Iron Dampier – China Navigation Co, Australia; VEB Mathias-Thesen-Werft, Wismar, 1981; 21,889dwt, 178m, 8ha, 6 x 25tn cr, 11,200bhp DMR-MAN (Tolerton)

In East Germany VEB Mathias-Thesen built a number of conbulkers including the *Iron Dampier* of 1981 (above), a four-hold, eight-hatch ship fitted with six 25tn paired cranes and equipped to carry 863 TEUs. Barely a year after completion as the *Palapur* for Hamburg owner F Laeisz she was sold to China Navigation Co as the *Kweilin*, and chartered in 1992 by Australian company Broken Hill Proprietary and modified to operate on BHP's trans-Tasman Sea liner service. The old Yugoslavia was prominent in both dry bulk and tanker construction, and this has continued now that the yards are in Croatia. Brodogradiliste contributed several ships to the Cast group (see "Specialised Types: Conbulkers"), including the 70,940dwt *Konavle* (below), which was completed at Rijeka in 1981 as the *Cast Caribou* and bought in 1992 by Atlantska Plovidba. Container capacity was 1466.

Konavle – Atlant Adria Corp. (Atlantska Plovidba dd), Croatia; Brodogradiliste "3 Maj," Rijeka, 1981; 70,940dwt, 234m, 7ha, 13,600bhp 3 Maj-Sulzer. (C Lous)

Uljanik – United Shipping Adriatic Inc (Uljanik Shipmanagement), Bahamas; Brodogradiliste "Uljanik," Pula, 1996; 44,377dwt, 183m, 5ha, 4 x 30tn cr, 11,665bhp Brodogradiliste-B&W. (Tolerton)

Spot the differences: Two modern bulk carriers of similar dimensions from Brodogradiliste yards, but with many visible differences. The Nassau-registered *Uljanik* (above) was delivered in 1996 from the Pula yard. Few oceangoing ships have both their name and port of registry identical on their sterns, but the *Split* of 1998 is one – built, inevitably, at Split. She is also unusual for her four 30tn hydraulic ram-luffing cranes, and she has a double bottom.

Split – Argo Maritime (Jadroplov dd), Croatia; Brodogradiliste "Split," Split, 1998; 42,584dwt, 187m, 5ha, 4 x 30tn cr, 9720bhp Tvornica DM Split-B&W. (Tolerton)

6

4

2

14 M

8

6

4

2

13 M

8

6

4

2

12 M

8

6

4

2

11 M

8

6

4

2

10 M

8

6

4

2

9 M

8

6

4

2

8 M

8

6

4

2

7 M

8

6

4

2

6 M

8

6

4

Delphic Miracle – Kalimnian Shipping Co (Carras Shipping Co, Piraeus), Liberia; Hitachi Zosen, Innoshima, 1961; 21,181dwt, 176m, 6ha, 5 x 8tn cr, 8750bhp Hitachi-B&W. (Tolerton)

CHAPTER SEVENTEEN

JAPANESE-BUILT HANDYSIZE BULK CARRIERS

Handysize ships make up more than two-thirds of the world bulk fleet, and Japan's shipyards have been the largest contributors. An early example was the *Delphic Miracle* of 1961 (left). More streamlined than bulk carriers were to be subsequently, she was a 21,181dwt ship from Hitachi Zosen for Greek owner Kalimnian Shipping Co. Vessels like this were soon superseded by handysize ships of considerably greater deadweight capacity on similar dimensions, and with more powerful cargo-handling gear. She went to Chinese breakers in 1984.

Shin Hsing – Karson Navigation Corp (Oak Steamship Co, Hong Kong), Taiwan; Kure Zosensho, Kure, 1966; 37,047dwt, 191m, 7ha, 16 x 5tn der, 11,200bhp IHI-Sulzer. (Tolerton)

Fitted with sixteen 5tn derricks and typifying what American seamen call a "stick ship," the *Shin Hsing* was built in 1966 for Yamashita-Shinnihon Kisen KK by Kure Zosensho as the *Shinnichi Maru*. After also trading as the *Shin Shin* from 1980, she became the *Shin Hsing* in 1982 as a Taiwanese-flag unit of the fleet controlled by Hong Kong owner Oak Steamship Co, and went to shipbreakers at her home port, Kaohsiung, in 1985.

Pergamos – Mercury Shipping Co (N J Goulandris, London), Greece; Sanoyasu Dockyard, Osaka, 1972; 17,605dwt, 147m, 5ha, 4 x 10tn cr, 9000bhp Sumitomo-Sulzer. (Tolerton)

Japanese builders were quick to offer standard designs and one of the first was the Sanoyasu Dockyard, Osaka, with a portfolio of vessels (all relatively small compared with today's handysizes) by the mid-1960s. The 17,602dwt *Pergamos* (above) was a 1972 Sanoyasu completion for London-Greek owner N J Goulandris, registered at the Goulandris home port, Andros. A typical logship of the 1970s with the trademark goalpost masts and stanchions was the *Maritime Joy* of 1976 (bottom) from Shikoku Dockyard. Built as the *Wakatake Maru* for Dainichi Kaiun KK, *Maritime Joy* was this ship's fourth name when she joined the fleet of Frank Tsao's International Maritime Carriers of Hong Kong under the Panamanian flag. The TAB initials on the sides of IMC ships in its Transasia Bulk pool always caused some mirth in New Zealand ports – TAB also being the initials of the state betting agency.

Maritime Joy – Hibernia Navigation Co (International Maritime Carriers, Hong Kong), Panama; Shikoku Dockyard, Takamatsu, 1976; 17,529dwt, 148m, 4ha, 4 x 25tn der, 8000bhp Mitsubishi. (Tolerton)

Star Castor – Mohawk Shipping Corp (Pegasus Shipping Enterprises, Piraeus), Greece; Hakodate Dock, Hakodate, 1973; 27,469dwt, 177m, 5ha, 4 X 15tn cr, 12,000bhp IHI-Sulzer. (Tolerton)

Cranes quickly proved their worth over derricks, particularly for grain and mineral cargoes, and the *Star Castor* (top), one of two sisters built by Hakodate Dock Co for leading London-Greek owners Rethymnis & Kulukundis to operate for Star Shipping, had four 15tn cranes serving five hatches. The rapid success of Japanese standard production was illustrated by the *Star Centaurus* of 1977 (bottom) from Mitsui Engineering and Shipbuilding. Also one of two sisters for R&K, she was a more sophisticated version of Mitsui's 30,000dwt standard bulk carrier of which 20 had already been built, and state of the art then. Drawing on their wide experience in the tramp trades, R&K stipulated extensive machinery automation, advanced navigational aids including automatic position finding, weather fax receiver, and anti-collision radar, and pollution avoidance equipment. In her cargo sections the configuration of the *Star Centaurus* was now fairly universal for the handysize bulker, topside and wing double-bottom tanks for ballast, which could also be carried in fore and aft peak tanks. Double-bottom tanks beneath holds two to six carried fuel which gave the ship a range of 14,000 miles. Hatch covers were chain-operated driven by electric motors, and the five 20tn cranes were on tall pedestals to accommodate timber cargoes.

Star Centaurus – Centaurus Shipping Corp (Rethymnis & Kulukundis, London), Greece; Mitsui, Chiba, 1977; 33,170dwt, 179m, 6ha, 5 x 20tn cr, 13,100bhp Mitsui-B&W. (Tolerton)

Nomadic Duchess – A/S Rederiet Odfjell (Nomadic Management AS), Norway; Mitsui, Ichihara, 1979; 35,105dwt, 179m, 5ha, 4 x 25tn cr, 11,200bhp Mitsui-B&W. (Tolerton)

The *Nomadic Duchess* of 1979 was another Mitsui completion of similar dimensions, but with five holds served by four 25tn cranes compared with the six and five of the *Star Centaurus*. Built as the *World Youth* for Sir Yue-Kong Pao's World-Wide Shipping, she had four more names before becoming the *Nomadic Duchess* on the Norway International Ship register in 1992, owned by A/S Rederiet Odfjell.

Vladimir Gavrilov – Black Sea Shipping Co, USSR; Nippon Kokan, Shimizu, 1977; 35,271dwt, 177m, 6ha, 5 x 15tn cr, 14,000bhp Sumitomo-Sulzer. (Tolerton)

Nippon Kokan built nine sisters for Kristian Jebsen companies in the 70s, three being sold to the USSR in 1983. The *Vladimir Gavrilov*, originally the British-flag *Borgnes* operated by Jebsens (UK) Ltd, was one of Soviet trio. A projecting wheelhouse, not visible in this view, was a feature of the design. Untypically for their day, the Jebsen ships had enclosed lifeboats.

Talisman – Wilbulk I K/S (BCP Shipmanagement, London), Norway; Imabari, Marugame, 1977; 23,757dwt, 159m, 4ha, 3 x 25tn cr, 1 x 25tn der, 10,650bhp Mitsubishi. (Tolerton)

Two 1970s Japanese bulkers which operated for prominent European ship owners were the *Talisman* of 1977 (above) and the *Hans Oldendorff* of 1979 (below). The former, built as the Japanese *Garza Star*, was one of many similar ships completed by Imabari Zosen, one of the bulk carrier builders in the second tier of the Japanese shipbuilding industry, and became an orphan addition to the fleet of leading Norwegian owner Wilh.Wilhelmsen in 1988. The cargo-handling gear embraced three cranes and one derrick, all 25tn. Under her original name the four-hatch vessel had been abandoned in the North Pacific in 1985 after developing a list, but was towed to Seattle. She was sold to Panamanian owners after less than three years in Wilhelmsen colours. Built by Kochi Jyuko KK as the *Flora Island* in 1979, the *Hans Oldendorff* joined German owner Egon Oldendorff's large fleet of bulk carriers on a long bareboat charter in 1989. She is equipped with four 25tn derricks for her four holds.

Hans Oldendorff – First Marine Shipping Pte, Singapore; Kochi Jyuko, Kochi, 1979; 22,531dwt, 151m, 4ha, 4 x 25tn der, 9300bhp Mitsubishi. (Tolerton)

Giovanni – Wales Shipping Co (Gestion Maritime SAM, Monte Carlo), Liberia; IHI, Aioi, 1977; 37,680dwt, 187m, 5ha, 1 x 25tn & 3 x 15tn cr, 11,400bhp IHI-Sulzer.

Ishikawajima-Harima is famous for its successful series of general cargo and bulk standard designs, and more than 30 of the 37,000dwt Future 32s like the *Giovanni* (top) and *Rosina Topic* (centre), both Liberian flag, were built. While the former, one of the first completions in 1977, had three 15tn and one 25tn cranes, the latter had four 25tn cranes to serve her five holds. From this design evolved the even more successful flush-decked Future 32As like the Cypriot *Aliacmon River* (bottom). IHI completed the first 32As in 1984 and orders for Sanko dominated early production. Vessels like the *Aliacmon River*, completed in 1994 as the *Glorious Future*, were still being built 10 years later. (See also The Sanko Ships)

Rosina Topic – Altop Navigation Corp (Marfin Management SAM, Monte Carlo), Liberia; IHI, Aioi, 1980; 37,244dwt, 187m, 5ha, 4 x 25tn cr, 12,000bhp IHI-Sulzer.

Aliacmon River – Sithonia Shipping Co (Acomarit UK), Cyprus; IHI, Chita, 1994; 38,858dwt, 180m, 5ha, 4 x 25tn cr, 6715bhp Diesel United-Sulzer. (All Tolerton)

Waglan Light – Hong Kong Navigation, Panama; Watanabe Zosen, Hakata, 1982; 21,355dwt, 152m, 4ha, 3 x 25tn cr, 1 x 25tn der, 8040bhp Mitsubishi-Sulzer. (Tolerton)

Hong Kong owners have become increasingly important players in dry bulk shipping in the past two decades, and by the end of 2001 more than half the fleet of nearly 63 million dwt controlled by Hong Kong companies comprised bulk carriers. One of its most interesting fleets is that of Santana Shipping Services, with its ships named after lighthouses and its handsome funnel with crossed flags carrying the initials of its directors Jan Loyning and William Swigart. Appropriately named after a Hong Kong seamark, the *Waglan Light* (top), acquired by Santana in 1995, was built in 1982 by Watanabe Zosen and one of a very large group of similar 21,000dwt ships from this builder and Imabari Zosen. A larger Hong Kong fleet, whose red and gray diagonally divided funnel provides another particularly distinctive marking, is that of Frank Tsao's IMC Shipping (previously International Maritime Carriers). IMC's *Maritime Fidelity* (bottom) was completed in 1984 as the *Gold Mount* by Imabari – one of dozens of handysizes built by Imabari during the decade. The *Maritime Fidelity* was lost off Singapore in 1999. Panamanian-registered four-hatch loggers, the *Waglan Light* and *Maritime Fidelity* both have a 25tn derrick to serve No.1 hatch, plus three cranes – all 25tn for the former and 30tn for the latter.

Maritime Fidelity – Kariba Navigation Co (IMC Shipping Co Pte, Singapore), Panama; Imabari Zosen, Imabari, 1984; 25,406dwt, 159m, 4ha, 3 x 30tn cr, 1 x 25tn der, 7000bhp Mitsui-B&W. (Tolerton)

Federal Manitou – K/S Consenus Star 11 (Det Nordenfjeldske D/S), Norway; Hitachi Zosen, Innoshima, 1983; 28,192dwt, 178m, 5ha, 4 x 25tn der, 7999bhp Hitachi-B&W. (Tolerton)

Among a range of designs up to the largest tankers, Hitachi Zosen also offered smaller bulk carrier designs. Norwegian owner Det Nordenfjeldske D/S's *Federal Manitou* (her fourth name after being built as the *Kalliopi II*), above, was completed in 1983 as one of Hitachi's first 28,000dwt standards. The five-hatch vessel had four 25tn cranes, and a relatively high listed speed of 16.75kn. A slightly larger vessel from Hitachi was the Greek-flag *Star Michalis* of 1985 (below), also with five holds and four 25tn cranes – and one of the many bulk carriers, both conventional and open hatch, operating for Star Shipping. She was built as the *Ocean Glory* and became part of the fleet of Rethymnis & Kulukundis, which chartered many vessels to Star Shipping, in 1992.

Star Michalis – Pequot Shipping Corp (Rethymnis & Kulukundis, London), Greece; Hitachi, Maizuru, 1985; 37,574dwt, 185m, 5ha, 4 x 25tn cr, 8670bhp Hitachi-B&W. (Tolerton)

Sea Tiger – Aral Shipping Co (Glafki (Hellas) Maritime Co), Greece; IHI, Tokyo, 1973; 22,631dwt, 164m, 5ha, 5 x 10tn cr, 8000bhp IHI-Pielstick. (Tolerton)

As well as the Future standards, IHI had great success with its 22,000dwt Fortune standard design. More than 60 were built at IHI yards during the 1970s and early 80s, many for Greek owners including the *Sea Tiger* of 1973 from the Tokyo yard, where the majority were built. The Fortune had five 10tn Universal Cargo Gear cranes and the option of car decks in five tiers in all five holds, enabling 1500 cars to be carried, or car decks in holds two and four, and was designed for a crew of 27. Fuel consumption was 29tns a day.

Turicum – Bulk Shipping (Switzerland) AG (J&W Shipping, Zurich), Switzerland; Oshima Shipbuilding, Oshima, 1995; 47,640dwt, 189m, 5ha, 4 x 25tn cr, 9976bhp Kawasaki-B&W. (Tolerton)

The "Swiss navy" is no joke – Switzerland has a large merchant fleet. However, the Swiss connection for the *Turicum* (the Latin name for Zurich) was confined to owner, flag, and port of registry when this photograph was taken in 1997, two years after her completion. The *Turicum* had a crew of 19 Filipinos, including the master, and two Burmese. The 47,640dwt ship was one of more than 50 similar-size five-hatch bulkers from Oshima Shipbuilding in the 1990s. Prominent are the electro-hydraulic grabs for unloading homogeneous cargoes.

117

Coral Gem – Sea Explorer Co (Gleamray Maritime Inc, Athens), Malta; Oshima, Oshima, 1995; 45,320dwt, 189m, 5ha, 4 x 30tn cr, 10,049bhp Mitsubishi. (Tolerton)

Several Japanese yards specialise in bulk carrier construction, but few to the extent of Oshima Shipbuilding, builder of the *Turicum*. A joint venture of Osaka Zosen and Sumitomo, Oshima launched its first ship in 1975 and had completed more than 300 bulk carriers quarter of a century later. The *Turicum* and *Coral Gem* (above), both of 1995, are representative of a very successful Oshima flushdecked standard design. The latter has a deadweight tonnage 1300 tonnes less, but more powerful 30tn cranes.

Iron Sturt – Broken Hill Pty Co, Australia; IHI, Kure, 1979; 22,093dwt, 161m, 4ha, 9000bhp IHI-Sulzer. (Tolerton)

An interesting representative of the smaller bulker output from Japanese yards is the gearless *Iron Sturt* of 1979, built by IHI for Australia's Broken Hill Proprietary and purchased by BHP in 1989 after a 10-year bareboat charter. The mid two of her four holds are long enough to carry 27m steel rails. She's carried a variety of bulk cargoes on the Australian coast, and after 25 years is still in service for BHP.

Pacsea – Pacific Coast Shipping Co (Lasco Shipping Co, Portland), Liberia; Minami-Nippon Zosen, Usuki; 1986; 26,986dwt, 174m, 5ha, 4 x 30tn cr, 7170bhp Mitsubishi. (Tolerton)

Minami-Nippon Zosen and Kurushima Dockyard have also been prolific constructors of bulkers. Built as the *Summer Breeze*, Lasco Shipping's *Pacsea* of 1986 (above) was sold along with two sisters for a top of the market price of US$38 million in 2004. Lasco of Portland, Oregon, was established in the early 60s by the Schnitzer family, prominent in the US steel industry, to ship its scrap metal, and its flag of convenience bulkers competed very successfully in the Pacific basin against the Eastern companies which dominate this sphere of bulker trading before the 23 ship Lasco fleet was sold to the Clipper group of the Bahamas for $200 million in December 2003. Representative of Kurushima's output is the *Azur* (below), completed in 1983 as the *Violet Islands* and one of a dozen similar vessels from this builder. The *Azur* operates for Monte Carlo-based Transocean Maritime Agencies.

Azur – Chase Finance Inc (Transocean Maritime Agencies SAM, Monte Carlo), St Vincent & the Grenadines; Kurushima Dockyard, Onishi, 1983; 37,092dwt, 189m; 5ha, 5 x 25tn cr, 8000bhp Mitsubishi. (Tolerton)

Tsuneishi Shipbuilding Co is another company most closely associated with bulk carrier construction, and has had enormous success with its five-hatch, 14kn TESS (Tsuneishi economical standard ship) series. More than 100 have been built to the TESS 40 (40,000dwt) and TESS 45 (45,000dwt) designs. The first TESS 40, the *Gleneagles*, was completed in 1984, and from it evolved the 45 – its increased deadweight supported by the same speed and fuel consumption as the 40. In 2000 Tsuneishi completed its first 52,000dwt TESS 52.

The TESS 45 *Great Peace* (below) was completed in 1996 for Worlder Shipping, one of the Hong Kong shipping companies whose fleet grew rapidly in the 1990s. An earlier version is the Taiwanese-owned *Grand Festival* (bottom) of 1993, on charter to Gearbulk. The names chosen by Hong Kong Chinese owners, usually with connotations of prosperity or virtue, occasionally lose something in their translation to English, as with another Worlder Shipping handysize, the immortal *Great Motion*.

Great Peace – Great Peace Shipping (Worlder Shipping), Hong Kong; Tsuneishi Shipbuilding, Numakuma, 1996; 45,259dwt, 185m, 5ha, 4 x 30tn cr, 11,300bhp Kawasaki-B&W. (Tolerton)

Grand Festival – Altringham Shipping, Panama; Tsuneishi, Numakuma, 1993; 43,620dwt, 177m, 5ha, 4 x 30tn cr, 9680bhp Mitsui-B&W. (Tolerton)

Ken Zui – Delica Shipping (Inui Steamship Co, Kobe), Panama; Saiki Jukogyo, Saiki, 1996; 23,564dwt, 154m, 4ha, 4 x 30tn cr, 6649bhp Mitsui-B&W. (Tolerton)

An interesting specialist among the handysize operators is the Japanese company Inui Steamship Co, an autonomous subsidiary of Mitsui OSK, which has specialised in the forestry products trades for more than 40 years. It has been particularly closely associated with New Zealand, carrying more than 80 per cent of that country's log and sawn timber exports in some years. Inui has continuously upgraded its fleet, with the *Ken Zui* of 1996 (above) and *Ken Ann Maru* of 1997 (below) typical of its modern tonnage. As well as the "Ken" ("sword") prefix, Inui ships are readily recognisable by their gray funnels with a red emblem on a white band. The *Ken Zui* is a 23,564dwt logger with four long hatches – and a "kamikaze" lifeboat – from Saiki Jukogyo, while the larger *Ken Ann Maru* is a five-hatch (three of them box-shaped semi-open hatch) ship from Onomichi Zosen. Both have four 30tn cranes.

Ken Ann Maru – Inui Steamship Co, Japan; Onomichi Zosen, Onomichi, 1997; 32,115dwt, 171m, 5ha, 4 x 30tn cr, 8640bhp Akasaka-Mitsubishi. (Tolerton)

Laurel Island – Yahata Trader SA (Yahata Kisen Co, Namikata), Panama; Imabari Zosen, Imabari, 1997; 26,516dwt, 169m, 5ha, 4 x 30tn cr, 7400bhp Akasaka-Mitsubishi. (Tolerton)

Two more modern five-hatch standard design logships – the *Laurel Island*, a 26,516dwt 1997 completion from Imabari (above), and the 31,727dwt *Crimson Forest* of 1999, one of a Hakodate Dock series of shallow draft loggers with holds 2, 3, and 4 double hull and 1 and 5 conventional topside and hopper bottom (below). The *Laurel Island*, which has four 30tn cranes, operates for Japan's Iino Lines. The *Crimson Forest*, one of many bulk carriers operating for NYK, had a short career under her original name, being renamed the *Pine Hurst* in 2001 by her owners. Hakodate, like Imabari, is one of the second tier Japanese builders specialising in bulk carriers, and after being one of the first to offer standard designs in the 1960s has been to the fore in this field ever since.

Crimson Forest – Diamond Camellia SA (MK Ship Management Co), Panama; Hakodate Dock, Hakodate, 1999; 31,727dwt, 176m, 5ha, 4 x 30tn cr, 9598bhp Akasaka-Mitsubishi. (Tolerton)

Dorthe Oldendorff – Kingston Maritime Corp, Liberia; Saiki Jukogyo (hull) and Onomichi Zosen, 1994; 21,711dwt, 157m, 4ha, 4 x 30tn cr, 6479bhp Akasaka-Mitsubishi. (Tolerton)

Onomichi and Saiki Jukogyo built a series of 22,000dwt ships in the 90s including six for Egon Oldendorff like the *Dorthe Oldendorff* of 1994 (above). Shallow draft and suitable for both grain and log cargoes, these Liberian-registered four-hatch vessels have four 30tn cranes – and provision for more than 500 TEUs. A German pioneer in bulk shipping in the 1950s, Egon Oldendorff of Lubeck has continued to flourish in these trades. In 2004 the company operated nearly 200 owned or chartered ships, most of them bulkers, and also owns Flensburger shipyard. Kanasashi is another builder to have been prominent in handysize bulk carriers with vessels like Lasco's 28,249dwt *Paclogger* (ex-*Sea Dream*) of 1996 (below).

Paclogger – Trans-Pacific Shipping Co (Lasco Shipping Co, Portland), Liberia; KK Kanasashi, Toyohashi, 1996; 28,249dwt, 169m, 5ha, 4 x 30tn cr, 7200bhp Mitsubishi. (Tolerton)

Tasman Sea – Bernard (BVI) (Pacific Basin Bulk Shipping), Hong Kong; Kanda Zosensho, Kawajiri, 2001; 28,456dwt, 170m, 5ha, 4 x 35tn cr, 6851bhp Kobe Hatsudoki-Mitsubishi. (Tolerton)

Both part of Hong Kong's huge bulk carrier fleet, the double-bottomed *Tasman Sea* of 2001 (above) from Kanda Kosensho and the *Mount Travers* of 2002 (below) from Imabari are representative of two highly successful modern 28,000dwt designs. Twenty-four Kanda 28s and 20 of Kanda's 32,000dwt version had been delivered by early 2004, while the *Mount Travers* was the latest of a very large class from Imabari. Both operate for Hong Kong-based Pacific Basin Shipping, a company whose name leaves no doubt about its raison d'etre. Pacific Basin's International Handybulk Carriers, a pool established in 2001, has developed into one of the major handysize pools.

Mount Travers – Kia Shipping (BVI) (IndoChina Shipmanagement), Hong Kong; Imabari, Imabari, 2002; 28,484dwt, 169m, 5ha, 4 x 30tn cr, 7953bhp Makita-B&W. (Tolerton)

Frontier Angel – Eternity Maritime SA, Panama; Shin Kurushima Dockyard, Onishi, 2001; 52,478dwt, 182m, 5ha, 4 x 30tn cr, 11,217bhp Akasaka-Mitsubishi. (Tolerton)

In recent years "handymax" designs – bulk carriers of 45,000 to 53,000dwt – have been offered by builders to cater to a demand for larger ships. Typical is the 52,478dwt Panamanian flag *Frontier Angel* (above), delivered at the end of 2001 from Shin Kurushima Dockyard as one of a series readily identifiable by their perforated superstructures. Also prominent among the handymaxs is a similar sized design from Sanoyas Hishino Meisho, which includes seven "Agios" ("holy") ships delivered in 2000-01 for the Navios group management company Levant Maritime International of Piraeus, like the *Agios Anastasios* (below). Equipped with five 30tn cranes (two of them twinned), she is flagged in the Marshall Islands – an increasingly popular flag for bulk operators. Ships to this design have been completed for several other owners.

Agios Anastasios – Dvtikos Shipping Co (Levant Maritime International, Piraeus), Marshall Islands; Sanoyas Hishino Meisho, Kurashiki, 2001; 52,061dwt, 189m, 5ha, 5 x 30tn cr, 11,869bhp Diesel United-Sulzer. (Tolerton)

Top Sugar – Top Sugar Maritime (Top Glory Shipping Co, Hong Kong), Liberia; Oshima, Oshima, 1998; 29,952dwt, 170m, 5ha, 4 x 30tn cr, 7286bhp Kawasaki-B&W. (Tolerton)

The most notable development in bulk carriers in recent years has been the advent of double hull construction, in which bulker specialist Oshima Shipbuilding led the way in cooperation with Hong Kong owners Ming Wah Shipping and Top Glory Shipping. The *Top Sugar* (above) of 1998 was its first 30,000dwt double hull bulk carrier, although outwardly a conventional enough logger. The five holds incorporate conventional hopper-shaped bottoms and saddle tanks – the topside tanks are smaller to offset the reduction in cargo space because of the double hull. Advocates of double hulls say that as well as safety advantages, the smooth-sided cargo holds, without frames projecting, assist cargo-handling and also inspection and maintenance. And, like the first double-skin tankers, they may well have the advantage of anticipating future regulatory requirements. The Maltese-flag *Papua* of 2003 (below) is one of six ships to Hakodate Dock's 31,800dwt double hull design to be delivered to the German owner Orion Schiffahrts.

Papua – Colosseo Maritime (Orion Schiffahrts, Hamburg), Malta; Hakodate Dock, Hakodate, 2003; 31,817dwt, 176m, 5ha, 4 x 30tn cr, 9001bhp Akasaka. (Tolerton)

4

2

14 M

8

6

4

2

13 M

8

6

4

2

12 M

8

6

4

2

11 M

8

6

4

2

10 M

8

6

4

2

9 M

8

6

4

2

8 M

8

6

4

2

7 M

8

6

4

2

6 M

8

6

4

CHAPTER EIGHTEEN

THE SANKO SHIPS

Few events have had a more dramatic impact on dry bulk shipping than Sanko Steamship Co's massive ordering spree of the early 1980s – and the company's resulting financial crisis. Sanko, probably the world's largest shipping company at that time and one of Japan's oldest, ordered at least 125 handysizes totaling more than 4 million dwt tonnes for delivery in 1984 to 1986. They ranged from 23,000 to 42,000dwt and were typically five hatch vessels with four 25tn cranes – rather more powerful than the norm on comparable-sized bulkers at this time. The scale of the ordering required the support of three major banks, and the orders were spread around 14 Japanese shipbuilders.

Huge debts and depressed freight rates forced Sanko to seek court protection in August, 1985. After it was restructured, some of the vessels remained in Sanko's ownership, some were chartered back, and some had been snapped up as bargains by foreign owners. In recent years ships from the Sanko building programme still made up a significant portion of the world's handysize fleet, and as the photographs in this section, show, the Sanko ships were invariably built as loggers. Sanko itself has long been re-established as one of the major dry bulk companies, operating a fleet of more than 80 in 2004, as well as tankers and LPG ships.

Two of the most readily-identifiable Sanko types are vessels like the *Sanko Poppy*, below, which was one of the ships to remain in Sanko ownership, and the *China Merchant*, which was launched as the *Sanko Gemini*, and *Sanko Cymbidium*, overleaf, top and bottom.

The *Sanko Poppy* is one of a group of seven with the superstructure conspicuously trunked around the funnel, delivered by Kanasashi and Sasebo. Many similar ships have also been built by Hakodate outside the Sanko programme. The pair overleaf are Future 32A standard designs from Ishikawajima-Harima. At least 18 Future 32As were ordered in the Sanko programme – the largest single group among 16 designs. Flush-decked and with the funnel offset to starboard, no bulk carriers are recognised more easily than these ships.

Sanko Poppy – Kiwi Maritime SA (The Sanko Steamship Co), Panama; Kanasashi, Toyohashi, 1985; 26,529dwt, 167m, 5ha, 4 x 25tn cr, 5865bhp Mitsui-B&W. (Tolerton)

China Merchant – Ningbo Coastal Lines (Fairmont Shipping Canada), Hong Kong; IHI, Aioi, 1986; 38,888dwt, 179m, 5ha, 4 x 25tn cr, 6800bhp IHI-Sulzer. (Tolerton)

Sanko Cymbidium – Cymbidium Maritime SA, Panama; IHI, Aioi, 1985; 38,888dwt, 180m, 5ha, 4 x 25tn cr, 6800bhp IHI-Sulzer. (Tolerton)

Sigana – Tschudi & Eitzen AS (Tschudi & Eitzen (India) Pvt), Panama; Mitsubishi, Nagasaki, 1985; 42,842dwt, 189m, 5ha, 4 x 25tn cr, 7965bhp Mitsubishi-Sulzer. (Tolerton)

After the IHI Future 32A order, the biggest order to one shipyard for one design went to Mitsubishi for twelve 42,800dwt vessels like the *Sigana* (above). Completed as *Sanko Gannet*, she was quickly renamed *Spring Gannet*, and then in 1998 became a Panamanian-flag unit of Norwegian owner Tschudi & Eitzen's fleet. Mitsubishi also received orders for two other groups of vessels, including six 27,600dwt ships like the *Torm Eastern* of 1986, below, which was launched as the *Sanko Solar* and took her fifth name when she began operating for the Danish shipowner D/S Torm in 1994. Concentrating on handysizes and Panamaxs, Torm and Tschudi & Eitzen have both helped to ensure that Scandinavian owners remain prominent in dry bulk shipping.

Torm Eastern – Peacehaven Shipping (Fortuna Navigation Co, Hong Kong), Panama; Mitsubishi, Nagasaki, 1986; 27,652dwt, 165m, 5ha, 4 x 25tn cr, 7730bhp Mitsubishi. (Tolerton)

Nego Wes – Handybulk Investors (No.3) (Wallem Shipmanagement), Hong Kong; Mitsubishi, Shimonoseki, 1984; 33,024dwt, 174m, 5ha, 4 x 25tn cr; 6570bhp Mitsubishi. (Tolerton)

A third group of half a dozen vessels from Mitsubishi comprised 33,000dwt vessels like the *Nego Wes* of 1984, above, which was the *Sanko Heritage* until 1995 when she joined the large fleet of long-established and prominent Hong Kong operator Wallem Shipmanagement. Wallem's yellow funnel incorporating Norway's national colours in a link to its founder is one of the most distinguished to be seen on bulk carriers, and as well as operating vessels of its own Wallem is a leading ship management company.

Mitsui contributed nine 41,500dwt ships like the *Serife* (below) to Sanko. This ship was built as the *Sanko Falcon* in 1984, becoming the *Spring Falcon* two years later with one of the changes of prefix that was typical during Sanko's restructuring. Turkish owners bought her in 1991 and renamed her *Serife*. Some, if not all, of this group were fitted with Mitsui's propeller duct intended to improve propulsion efficiency.

Serife – Bati Denizcilik Isletmesi SA, Turkey; Mitsui, Tamano, 1984; 41,544dwt, 182m, 5ha, 4 x 25tn cr; 8419bhp Mitsui-B&W. (Tolerton)

Reliance Trader – Reliance Maritime, Liberia; Sasebo, Sasebo, 1984; 37,692dwt, 188m, 5ha, 4 x 25tn cr, 6936bhp IHI-Sulzer. (Tolerton)

Springwood – Logan Sea Maritime (Soc. Anonyme Monegasque d'Administration Maritime et Aerienne, Monte Carlo), Panama; Kanasashi, Toyohashi, 1984; 37,694dwt, 188m, 5ha, 4 x 25tn cr, 8160bhp Hitachi-Sulzer. (Tolerton)

Telina – Orient Maritime SA (Eastern Shipping KK), Panama; Hitachi, Innoshima, 1984; 37,705dwt, 185m, 5ha, 4 x 25tn cr, 8600bhp Hitachi-B&W. (Tolerton)

A major group of ships in the Sanko programme was made up by fifteen 37,600dwt vessels from Kanasashi (seven) and Sasebo (eight).

The Liberian-flag *Reliance Trader* (previous page, top) was a 1984 Sasebo completion as the *Sanko Reliance* and after her change of name in 1986 continued to operate in Sanko's livery. Operating on charter as part of Danish shipowner J Lauritzen's large bulk carrier fleet, the *Springwood* (previous page, centre) was a 1984 Kanasashi completion. She was built as the *Sanko Hawk*, becoming the *Spring Hawk* in 1986, then the Panamanian-flag *Springwood* in 1993. Best-known for its reefers and Arctic ships, Lauritzen, which acquired its first bulk carrier in 1973, has become prominent in bulk shipping with a large fleet of mainly chartered ships.

Very similar to the above vessels were six ships from Hitachi Zosen including the *Telina* (previous page, bottom), which was completed as the *Sanko Amaryllis* in 1984. She dropped the Sanko prefix a year later, and became the Panamanian *Telina* (still in Sanko livery) in 1989.

The cadet ship Filipinas

One of the most unusual bulk carriers built in the 1980s was the 28,184dwt *Filipinas*, delivered to the National Maritime Polytechnics of Manila by Denmark's Aalborg Vaerft in July 1983. The *Filipinas* was also a cadet training ship, with facilities for 240 deck and engineer officer cadets and 18 teachers, and as well as classrooms and laboratories had a training bridge and training engine control room. The project envisaged the ship covering both her operation and student training costs trading between the Philippines and the US Gulf (sugar outwards and grain home), and she had two 20tn and three 10tn cranes.

Filipinas – National Maritime Polytechnics, Philippines; Aalborg Vaerft, Aalborg, 1983; 28,184dwt, 173m, 6ha, 2 x 20tn & 3 x 10tn cr, 13,051bhp Helsingor-B&W. (Tolerton)

4
2
14 M
8
6
4
2
13 M
8
6
4
2
12 M
8
6
4
2
11 M
8
6
4
2
10 M
8
6
4
2
9 M
8
6
4
2
8 M
8
6
4
2
7 M
8
6
4
2
6 M
8
6
4

CHAPTER NINETEEN

THE HITACHI PANAMAXS

The completion of the 75,115dwt *Spartia* by Hitachi Zosen in 2000 was a notable milestone for this shipbuilder. The *Spartia* was the 100th Panamax built by Hitachi, and the series has put the company foremost among builders of bulk carriers of this size.

Hitachi's first Panamax was the 60,542dwt *Blessing* for Hong Kong owners in 1969, and it developed its Panamax design through four "generations." The latest has a 23 per cent greater deadweight, 20 per cent greater hold capacity, and a 31 per cent improvement in fuel consumption on the early vessels. Hitachi's energy-saving "super stream propeller duct" contributes to the latter, the fourth generation vessels consuming 32.2 tonnes a day.

Its features typical of most Panamax designs, the Hitachi Mark 2 which contributed more than a third of the ships to the series was a 225m gearless bulk carrier with a deadweight of 61,300tn. The vessel had seven holds, steel side-rolling hatch covers, strengthening for ore cargoes, fuel consumption of about 36tn a day and a service speed of 14.5 knots. It was designed for a complement of 30, and the funnel casing was completely detached from the bridge-accommodation house to minimise vibration. A gantry stores crane separates the two.

Illustrated here are three Greek-owned Hitachi Zosen Panamaxs, which reflect the popularity the design quickly found with foreign ship owners. The 64,135wt *Thalia* (below) was a Mark 2 version built in 1982 as the *Maritime Baron* and acquired by the prominent Greek owner Lykiardopoulos's Neda Maritime Agency Co of Piraeus in 1989. The *Spartia* was also built for a Lykiardopoulos company.

Thalia – Seabay Shipping Corp (Neda Maritime Agency Co), Greece; Hitachi, Maizuru, 1982; 64,135dwt, 224m, 7ha, 13,800bhp Hitachi-B&W. (Tolerton)

Samjohn Spirit – Toxotis Shipping Co (Golden Flame Shipping SA), Greece; Hitachi, Maizuru, 1994; 71,730dwt, 223m, 7ha, 12,240bhp Hitachi-B&W. (Tolerton)

Two later Hitachi Panamaxs also for Greek owners were the 71,730dwt *Samjohn Spirit* of 1994, above, and 71,662dwt *Oinoussian Legend* of 1997, below. The name of the latter, incidentally, is a tribute to one of the most remarkable features of Greece's modern maritime history – the contribution of families from the tiny island of Oinoussai, near Chios. The tightly-knit Lemos, Pateras, Hadjipateras, Lyras, and Samonas families of Oinoussai eventually came to own a fleet of more than 500 ships from small beginnings with three of the families investing in their first steamer 100 years ago. The *Oinoussian Legend* is owned by a Lemos company and the *Samjohn Spirit* a Samonas vessel.

Oinoussian Legend – Legend Shipping Corp (Efploia Shipping Co SA), Greece; Hitachi, Maizuru, 1997; 71,662dwt, 223m, 7ha, 11,829bhp Hitachi-B&W. (Tolerton)

4
2
14 M
8
6
4
2
13 M
8
6
4
2
12 M
8
6
4
2
11 M
8
6
4
2
10 M
8
6
4
2
9 M
8
6
4
2
8 M
8
6
4
2
7 M
8
6
4
2
6 M
8
6
4

C.S.Pegasus – Caribstar Shipping SA (Chugoku Sogyo KK), Panama; Mitsui, Tamano, 1998; 77,663dwt, 229m, 5ha, 11,820bhp Mitsui-B&W. (Tolerton)

CHAPTER TWENTY

OTHER JAPANESE PANAMAX-TYPE DESIGNS

While the Hitachi Panamax has been particularly successful, Panamax designs feature in the portfolios of most Japanese shipyards. Nippon Kokan was one of the first builders to start series construction of Panamax types with ships like the rather inappropriately-named (although she does have a cruiser stern) *Beauteous*, below, built for the Showa Line in 1969 as *Shozui Maru*. The 59,410dwt ship went to Chinese breakers in 1992. At least one builder, Koyo Dockyard, persisted with cruiser sterns on Panamaxs well into the 1980s. As the vessels on the next pages show, much greater deadweight was achieved in later Panamaxs on the same overall length as the *Beauteous*. The 77,663dwt *C.S.Pegasus* of 1998 (opposite) from Mitsui is not quite a Panamax. With beam 4m greater, she was built as the *Energy Pegasus*, the first of three wide-beam coal carriers with five long double-skin holds for Mitsui OSK. She changed name in 2000 and is chartered to carry for Tohoku Electric Power. The photo shows her reinforced mooring equipment for winter cargo handling in Japan's more exposed ports.

Beauteous – Teh Hu Steamship Co, Taiwan; Nippon Kokan, Tsurumi, 1969; 59,410dwt, 227m, 7ho (11ha), 15,000bhp Uraga-Sulzer. (Tolerton)

Torm Tekla – Tekla Shipping Co (D/S Torm), Bahamas; Tsuneishi, Numakuma, 1993; 69,268dwt, 225m, 7ha, 12,120bhp Kawasaki-B&W. (Tolerton)

Tsuneishi is active in Panamax construction as it is with handysizes. The 69,268dwt *Torm Tekla* of 1993 (above), a Bahaman flag bulker in the fleet of Danish owner D/S Torm, is one of more than 40 standard ships like this from Tsuneishi. Suitable for all bulk cargoes including ore in alternate holds, these ships are typical Panamaxs – seven holds with topside shoulder tanks and hoppered bottom tanks, hydraulic motor-driven side-rolling steel hatch covers, and gearless. Fuel consumption is about 30tn a day. The 75,966dwt Panamanian *Santa Vitoria* of 2002 (below) updates the Tsuneishi Panamax, with greater capacity on the same hull dimensions as the *Torm Tekla* and a double bottom. The funnel shows she's part of the fleet of Italian drybulk operator Coeclerici, which in 2001 merged with the Livanos-owned Ceres Hellenic, the new Coeclerici Ceres fleet comprising 20 Capesizes and Panamaxs.

Santa Vitoria – Compania Flor de Vapores SA (Dia Marine Corp), Panama; Tsuneishi, Numakuma, 2002; 75,966dwt, 225m, 7ha, 16,680bhp Mitsui-B&W. (Tolerton)

CHAPTER TWENTY-ONE

SOUTH KOREAN-BUILT BULK CARRIERS

South Korea and Japan have been fierce rivals for the ranking of the world's top shipbuilding nation since Korea overhauled its rival across the Sea of Japan for the first time in 1993. In Korean yards, as in Japan, bulk carriers of all sizes make up a large portion of the output. In the late 1980s Hyundai Heavy Industries became the world's largest shipbuilder, and the *Federal Rhine* of 1977 was one of a group of Lakers for Fednav that made up a major early order from the west. The gearless 35,910dwt ship is pictured (opposite) as the *Steel Flower* after she was sold in 1993 to Panamanian owners. Daewoo Shipbulding, Hyundai's closest rival, built a dozen 47,300dwt bulkers like the *Hardwar* of 1986 (below) for the Shipping Corporation of India. The ship has five holds and five 25tn cranes.

Hardwar – Shipping Corporation of India, India; Daewoo, Okpo, 1986; 47,311dwt, 189m, 5ha, 5 x 25tn cr, 10,800bhp Korea HI-B&W. (Tolerton)

Eser Kaptanoglu – Gunes Gemicilik ve Tankercilik, Turkey; Hyundai, Ulsan, 1982; 37,227dwt, 186m, 5ha, 4 x 25tn cr, 10,901bhp Hyundai-B&W. (Tolerton)

As the South Korean-flag *Asia No.16,* the *Eser Kaptanoglu* (above) was completed in 1982 by Hyundai as the first of a series of a dozen or so ships to its "energy-saving handysize" 37,000dwt design. Moderate fuel consumption of 19.4tn a day was a selling point. Renamed *Hyundai No.16* two years later, she operated for Hyundai Merchant Marine Co until her sale to Turkish owners in 1995. She had five holds, four 25tn cranes, and provision for 750 TEUs. A larger design from Hyundai was the 45,112dwt *Wadi Al Natroon,* one of half a dozen similar ships for the National Navigation Co of Cairo. Also with five holds, this ship had four less powerful 15tn cranes, and fuel consumption of about 26tn a day.

Wadi Al Natroon – National Navigation Co, Egypt; Hyundai, Ulsan, 1985; 45,112dwt, 195m, 5ha, 4 x 15tn cr, 10,940bhp Hyundai-Sulzer. (Tolerton)

Mary F – Summer Shipping SA (Fairsky Shipping and Trading SA, Athens), Liberia; Daewoo, Okpo, 1996; 43,910dwt, 190m, 5ha, 4 x 30tn cr; 10,480bhp Korea HI-B&W. (Tolerton)

Another more modern class of about 10 Daewoo vessels with similarities to the SCI ships like the *Hardwar* is represented by the *Mary F* of 1996 (above), a Liberian-flag vessel of the Athens fleet of Fairsky Shipping and Trading. The main difference is four cranes instead of five – on the *Mary F*, they are 30tn ones.

Hyundai completed eight 43,000dwt flush-decked ships like the *Pacific Mayor* of 1995 (below) for the Hyundai Merchant Marine Co, and five more for the Malaysia International Shipping Corporation. The ship had five holds and four 25tn cranes. About a quarter of the world's bulk carrier fleet is, like this ship, under the flag of Panama – the most popular flag for bulk carriers.

Pacific Mayor – Meta Ship Co SA (Hyundai Merchant Marine Co), Panama; Hyundai, Ulsan, 1995; 43,176dwt, 185m, 5ha, 4 x 25tn cr, 10,576bhp Hyundai-B&W. (Tolerton)

Hanjin Calcutta – Korea French Banking Corp (Hanjin Shipping Co), South Korea; Hanjin, Pusan, 1997; 27,365dwt, 167m, 5ha, 4 x 30tn cr, 9050bhp Hyundai-B&W. (Tolerton)

Not surprisingly, the Hanjin Shipping Co has taken many ships from Hanjin Heavy Industries, the *Hanjin Calcutta* of 1997 (above) being one of a 27,300dwt series which also included vessels for Korean rival Pan Ocean Shipping. The *Hanjin Calcutta* is a five-hold bulker with four 30tn cranes, consuming about 25tns of fuel a day.

New Mariner – New Gulf BX Shipping (Pan Ocean Shipping Co), Panama; Hyundai, Ulsan, 1999; 31,024dwt, 176m, 5ha, 4 x 30tn cr, 8201bhp Hyundai-B&W. (Tolerton)

The *New Mariner* of 1999 is one of a five-hatch 31,000dwt logship class from Hyundai for domestic owner Pan Ocean Shipping Co. Established in the 1960s, this company entered dry bulk shipping with the new 19,014dwt *Pan-Korea* in 1972, and in 2004 owned or chartered more than 60 bulkers. While holds 1 and 5 are conventional hopper-type, the other three are box-shaped, and the ship has a double bottom and double skin sides.

Achilles – South Bulk Carriers (Transocean Maritime Agencies, Monte Carlo), Liberia; Hyundai, Ulsan, 1989; 68,772dwt, 225m, 7ha, 11,030bhp Hyundai-B&W. (Tolerton)

Two versions of Hyundai's Panamax design: The 68,772dwt Liberian flag *Achilles* of 1989 (above) and the 75,464dwt Greek flag *Anangel Enosis* of 1995 (below). Both are 225m 14kn vessels with seven holds, the former part of the small bulk carrier fleet operated by Transocean Maritime Agencies of Monte Carlo until sold in 2003 to become the *Greta R* under the Burmese flag, and the latter one of the many ships with the handsome cloverleaf funnel of Anangel Shipping Enterprises. The Angelicoussis company, domiciled until recently at that famous shipping address, the Akti Miaouli in Piraeus, was one of the first Greek ship owners to be publically listed in the USA.

Anangel Enosis – Caspian Sea Maritime (Anangel Shipping Enterprises SA, Piraeus), Greece; Hyundai, Ulsan, 1995; 75,464wt, 225m, 7ha, 13,889bhp Hyundai-B&W. (Tolerton)

Great Glory – Great Glory Shipping (Worlder Shipping), Hong Kong; Halla, Samho, 1997; 73,251dwt, 224m, 7ha, 10,949bhp Hyundai-B&W. (Tolerton)

Two Panamax design from other Korean builders – the *Great Glory* (above) from Halla Engineering and Heavy Industries was a double-bottomed 1997 addition to the fast-growing fleet of Worlder Shipping of Hong Kong, and the *Global Fortune* (below), owned by Pan Ocean Shipping but operating here on charter to Japan's Showa Line, came from Daewoo in 1984.

Global Fortune – Pan Ocean Shipping Co, South Korea; Daewoo, Okpo, 1984; 64,964dwt, 224m, 7ha, 13,000bhp Daewoo-B&W. (Tolerton)

Liberty Sun – Liberty Shipping Group (Liberty Maritime Corp), USA; Hyundai, Ulsan, 1986; 63,400dwt, 225m, 7ha, 4 x 15tn cr, 15,880bhp Hyundai-B&W. (Kevin Moore)

Panamaxs are generally gearless, and bulkers flying the Stars and Stripes in ocean trades are also uncommon, which makes the *Liberty Sun* of 1986 from Hyundai a notable ship on two counts. Built as the *Aspen*, the ship has four rather modest 15tn cranes, is fitted to carry 500 TEUs, and is one of a group of five from Hyundai registered in New York and operating for Liberty Maritime Corporation, which with eight or so vessels has the largest US-flag oceangoing bulk fleet. The *Liberty Sun* is pictured arriving at Durban.

Marijeannie – Marijeannie Shipping Co (Chandris Hellas), Greece; Daewoo, Okpo, 2001; 74,410dwt, 225m, 7ha, 14,900bhp Korea HI-B&W. (Tolerton)

A modern Panamax from Daewoo is the *Marijeannie*, which was completed in 2001 as the *SA Gladiator* – one of the last vessels ordered by the South African Marine Corporation. All seven holds are of identical dimensions. She was sold to Chandris in 2003.

Ibis Arrow – Gearbulk Shipowning (Kristian Gerhard Jebsen Skipsrederi), Bahamas; Samsung, Koje, 1986; 42,497dwt, 187m, 7ha, 2 x 35tn gantry cr, 8400bhp Hyundai-B&W. (Tolerton)

An important order for Korean yards in the 1980s, shared by Samsung and Hyundai, came from Gearbulk for 11 open hatch ships like the *Ibis Arrow* (above). Double skin sides, bow thrusters, and capacity for 1392 TEUs were among the features of the design. Perhaps it is difficult to find anything of the traditional romance of ships and the sea in most bulk carriers, but the *Anderso* (below) offered a hint in her ancestry. Another open hatch ship which also served Gearbulk, she was a 1978 completion from Hyundai in a six-ship order from two Finnish owners, and designed to carry pulp, newsprint, or containers in four box holds. The 16,797dwt *Anderso* was one of two for Gustaf Erikson, and like Erikson's famous tall ships was registered at Mariehamn in the Aland Islands. While Erikson is remembered for operating the last commercial sail fleet, it is perhaps overlooked that he bought his first steamers as early as 1920 – 22 years before his last sailer. Captain Eljer Wahlsten, master of the *Anderso* in early 1980s, had sailed on the four-masted barques *Viking* and *Moshulu* before World War Two and was believed to be the last Cape Horn sailor at sea as a master.

Anderso – Gustaf Erikson, Finland; Hyundai, Ulsan, 1978; 16,797dwt, 163m, 4ha, 2 x 30tn cr, 9300bhp Kawasaki-MAN. (Tolerton)

6

4

2

14 M

8

6

4

2

13 M

8

6

4

2

12 M

8

6

4

2

11 M

8

6

4

2

10 M

8

6

4

2

9 M

8

6

4

2

8 M

8

6

4

2

7 M

8

6

4

2

6 M

8

6

4

CHAPTER TWENTY-TWO

CHINESE-BUILT BULK CARRIERS

The dominance of Japan and South Korea in bulk carrier construction and shipbuilding generally is now being eroded by China. As relatively unsophisticated ships, bulk carriers have inevitably been targeted in the construction programmes of countries finding their feet in this industry. China's first large ship for export was a bulk carrier, the *Regent Tampopo*, from Dalian Shipyard in 1981. Its shipbuilding industry has developed rapidly since then to rank behind only its two Asian neighbours, and plans for even greater expansion point to China overhauling them in a few years.

Bulker construction has evolved from handysizes to Panamaxs, and another milestone came in June 2003 with the delivery of the first large Capesize bulker from a Chinese yard. The 175,526dwt Dunkirkmax *CSK Fortune* for Hong Kong's Tai Chong Cheang Steamship Co was also the first vessel from the new Shanghai Waigaoqiao Shipbuilding, the first ship with MacGregor roll-up side-rolling hatch covers, and dubbed the "Green Cape" design for environmental protection features including double-hull bunker tanks.

One of the successes of China's handysize construction programme has been a series of log ships like the 27,827dwt *Torm Arawa* of 1997 (below) for various owners from Shanghai's Hudong Shipyard. Part of the charter fleet operating for D/S Torm of Denmark, the Liberian-flag *Torm Arawa* has five holds and four 30tn cranes.

Torm Arawa – Southern Light Shipping (Thome Ship Management, Singapore), Liberia; Hudong, Shanghai, 1997; 27,827dwt, 174m, 5ha, 4 x 30tn cr, 8414bhp Hudong-B&W. (Tolerton)

Selinda – Zehnte Oceania Schiffahrt GmbH (Transocean Shipmanagement GmbH, Hamburg), Liberia; Bohai, Huludao, 2001; 28,107dwt, 169m, 5ha, 4 x 30tn cr, 9250bhp Yichang-Sulzer. (Tolerton)

Also building handysizes is the Bohai Shipyard in northern Liaoning province, its output including the logger design represented by the 28,107dwt *Selinda* (above). This double-bottomed bulker is one of four similar Bohai ships in the fleet of German operator Transocean Shipmanagement, associated with Deutsche Afrika-Linien and John T Essberger. The advantages of KG financing and a dash of enterprise have kept Germany prominent in areas of shipping which some of their former West European maritime rivals have relinquished. Guangzhou Shipyard International has built a series of handysizes like the 26,517dwt *Althea* (below), completed in 1995 as the *Handy Althea*. Part of the large fleet managed by Anglo-Eastern Ship Management of Hong Kong, she's a five-hold logship.

Althea – Moor Loggers Corp (Anglo-Eastern Ship Management), Hong Kong; Guangzhou Shipyard, Guangzhou, 1995; 26,517dwt, 168m, 5ha, 4 x 30tn cr, 8258bhp Hudong-B&W. (Tolerton)

Federal Schelde – Lake St Clair (Anglo-Eastern Ship Management), Barbados; Jiangnan Shipyard, Shanghai, 1997; 34,372dwt, 199m, 6ha, 3 x 30tn cr, 11,640bhp Mitsui-B&W. (Tolerton)

With a history going back to 1865, Jiangnan Shipyard in Shanghai is China's oldest. In the 1920s it built Yangtze gunboats for the US Navy, and today is a leader in Chinese shipbuilding with a varied output that includes gas and oil tankers and container ships. The *Federal Schelde* of 1997 (above) was the last ship in a notable order for it of six Lakers for the Fednav group of Montreal, which were state of the art for oceangoing vessels designed to navigate the St Lawrence Seaway and Great Lakes, and, needless to say, ice-strengthened. Other Jiangnan completions include 45,300dwt ships, like the Swiss-flag *Unterwalden* of 1996 (below) for Massoel Gestion Maritime. Fuel consumption is 30tn a day.

Unterwalden – Massocean SA (Massoel Gestion Maritime SA), Switzerland; Jiangnan, Shanghai, 1996; 45,300dwt; 190m, 5ha, 4 x 30tn cr, 11,583bhp Shanghai Diesel-Sulzer. (Tolerton)

China Pride – Trans-Pacific Shipping Co (Lasco Shipping Co, Portland), Liberia; Jiangnan, Shanghai, 1990; 64,619dwt, 225m, 7ha, 12,850bhp Dalian Marine-B&W. (Tolerton)

Jiangnan has also enjoyed success with its Panamax designs. An early Panamax completion of note was the 64,619dwt *China Pride* (above) in 1990 for the Lasco company Trans-Pacific Shipping, and one of the first Chinese Panamaxs. As well as similar ships for Lasco, Jiangnan has built more than a dozen for other owners, domestic and foreign. The 74,000dwt, seven-hatch *Guang Ming Feng* (below) was completed by Jiangnan in 2002, and is one of four that were the largest Panamaxs completed in China. She was built for China Shipping, which since its formation as a merger of the three largest domestic shipping companies in 1997 has become a growing force in international shipping, although it has some way to go to catch China's giant, COSCO.

Guang Ming Feng – China Shipping (Group) Co, China; Jiangnan, Shanghai, 2002; 74,000dwt, 225m, 7ha, 13,867bhp Shanghai Shipyard-B&W. (Tolerton)

Wan Shou Shan – China Shipping International Intermodal Co, China; Dalian New Shipyard, Dalian, 1989; 39,837dwt, 195m, 6ha, 11,110bhp Dalian Marine-Sulzer. (Tolerton)

The Dalian New Shipyard was developed as the biggest, most modern yard of the China State Shipbuilding Corporation, and one of its early completions was the 39,837dwt *Wan Shou Shan* (above) of 1989 for China Shipping. The yard has also produced more sophisticated tonnage like the 51,468dwt *Penguin Arrow* (below) of 1997, one of eight open hatch, double-sided vessels for Gearbulk. *Penguin Arrow* has two 40tn gantry cranes serving 10 holds. The weather canopy protecting the cranes is a feature of these "fifth generation" ships for Gearbulk, but other features remain unchanged through a long series of open-hatch ships from two decades – Nassau-registry, Gearbulk's rather forbidding livery, the gantry cranes, and the characteristic knuckle at the bows to allow the cranes to serve No.1 hold.

Penguin Arrow – Gearbulk Shipowning (Kristian Gerhard Jebsen Skipsrederi), Bahamas; Dalian New Shipyard, Dalian, 1997; 51,468dwt, 199m, 10ha, 2 x 40tn gantry cr, 15,662bhp Dalian Marine-B&W. (Tolerton)

Ning An 7 – COSCO Shanghai, China; Guangzhou Shipyard, Guangzhou, 1993; 36,019dwt, 185m, 5ha, 9136bhp 2 x Yichang-B&W. (Tolerton)

The Guangzhou-built *Ning An 7* (above) is one of a series of similar twin screw, twin-engined bulk carriers from Guangzhou and Bohai for COSCO. Relatively shallow draught is a feature of some Chinese vessels built for domestic operation carrying cargoes like coal to terminals on China's rivers and estuaries. The *Ning An 7* draws 10m on overall length of 185m and 32m beam. Another example of Chinese handysize bulkers for domestic ownership is the *An Ping 6* from Shanghai Shipyard for China Shipping. The raked lattice masts are a distinctive feature of this ship, one of a group of similar bulkers from the Shanghai and Jiangnan yards.

An Ping 6 – Marisburg SA (China Shipping (HK) Marine Co), China; Shanghai Shipyard, Shanghai, 1987; 38,944dwt, 195m, 6ha, 3 cr, 12,960bhp Shanghai Diesel-Sulzer. (Tolerton)

6

4

2

14 M

8

6

4

2

13 M

8

6

4

2

12 M

8

6

4

2

11 M

8

6

4

2

10 M

8

6

4

2

9 M

8

6

4

2

8 M

8

6

4

2

7 M

8

6

4

2

6 M

8

6

4

CHAPTER TWENTY-THREE
OTHER ASIAN-BUILT BULK CARRIERS

Bulk carrier construction in Asia is not confined to the big three. Taiwan has also been a significant builder, and now the Philippines, where Tsuneishi set up a yard at Cebu in 1994, and Vietnam, where state shipbuilder Vietnam Ship Industry Corporation's yards at Haiphong and Halong will deliver its first orders for the UK Graig group in 2006, are also starting to make their mark. Representative of modern Taiwanese construction are the handysize and the Panamax ships pictured below. Although Singapore-registered, the 45,194dwt *Asian Glory* of 1996 from China Shipbuilding, Keelung, was built for Taiwan's largest bulk carrier operator, U-Ming Marine Transport, and is one of at least seven ships completed to this design. The 73,035dwt Swiss-flag *Celerina* of 1999 from China Shipbuilding's Kaohsiung yard is part of the Suisse-Atlantique fleet.

Asian Glory – U-Ming Marine Transport (Singapore) Pte, Singapore; China SB, Keelung, 1996; 45,194dwt, 189m, 5ha, 4 x 30tn cr, 10,499bhp Hitachi-B&W. (Tolerton)

Celerina – Oceana Shipping AG (Suisse-Atlantique Soc. de Nav. Maritime SA), Switzerland; China SB, Kaohsiung, 1999; 73,035dwt, 224m, 7ha, 11,220bhp Samsung-Sulzer. (Tolerton)

Nordholm – Orient Hakusan Shipping SA (Misuga Kaiun Co), Panama; Tsuneishi (Cebu), Balamban, 2000; 45,526dwt, 186m, 5ha, 4 x 30tn cr, 9749bhp Mitsui-B&W. (Tolerton)

An early completion in the Philippines from Tsuneishi's Cebu yard was the *Nordholm* of 2000. Danish operator D/S Norden (in which fellow Copenhagen shipowner Torm has a 30 per cent holding) started as a ship owner in 1871, but although it was operating about 100 bulk carriers in 2003, none were Norden-owned. Its vessels are all chartered long-term with a purchase option like the Panamanian-flag *Nordholm*, or time-chartered. The Cebu yard, in which the Aboitiz group is a partner, aims to complete about seven ships, mainly 52,00dwt bulkers, each year.

Apj Shalin – Surrendra Overseas, India; Cochin Shipyard, Cochin, 1989; 76,640dwt, 245m, 9ha, 19,079bhp Cegielski-Sulzer. (Tolerton)

The *Apj Shalin* was built for prominent Indian shipowner Surrendra Overseas of Kolkata by India's most successful builder, Cochin Shipyard, which has improving credentials as a builder of bulkers and tankers. Launched in 1986, this 76,640dwt, nine-hold Panamax was not completed until three years later. The "Apj" prefix in the Surrendra fleet, incidentally, comes from the initials of the group's founder.

4

2

14 M

8

6

4

2

13 M

8

6

4

2

12 M

8

6

4

2

11 M

8

6

4

2

10 M

8

6

4

2

9 M

8

6

4

2

8 M

8

6

4

2

7 M

8

6

4

2

6 M

8

6

4

"SERIOUSLY DEFICIENT" – THE DERBYSHIRE, THE SHIPS OF SHAME, AND BULK CARRIER SAFETY

Oil tankers have been under intense international scrutiny since the *Torrey Canyon* ran onto the Seven Stones Reef in March 1967, spilling thousands of tonnes of oil to coat the Cornish coast in a black tide.

It is only in the past two decades that bulk carrier safety has become anything like a similar issue, and even today it is more a concern for maritime specialists than for the general public, which by contrast is familiar with the havoc wrought to the environment by the loss of tankers like the *Torrey Canyon*, *Exxon Valdez*, *Braer*, and *Prestige*.

There is one major difference between tanker disasters and bulk carrier disasters. When tankers are lost, it is often the environment that is the worst victim. When bulk carriers, often carrying heavy ore cargoes, are lost, it is seafarers – and their families – that suffer most.

More than 2700 died in bulk carriers lost between 1971 and 1994. The cynic might conclude that the deaths of Filipino and Chinese seafarers on ships flagged in Liberia or Panama and owned in Hong Kong, Piraeus, or New York might have received considerably more attention had they been accompanied by destruction of the seashore and wildlife, too.

Bulk carrier safety issues started to receive closer attention, at least in the English-speaking world, as a result of the loss of the four-year-old British OBO *Derbyshire* in 1980 and through the Australian Ships of Shame report in December, 1992.

The disappearance of Bibby's *Derbyshire* became the subject of two inquiries and well-organised agitation by relatives, unions, and experienced seafarers. It was far from an isolated bulk carrier disaster, but the loss of a modern, well-equipped British ship owned by a reputable company and the deaths of 44 people drew serious attention to concerns about bulk carrier safety.

The Ships of Shame report to the Australian federal parliament followed an inquiry chaired by Transport Minister Peter Morris after the loss of several large bulkers that had sailed from West Australian ports with ore cargoes, and galvanized authorities into action against substandard ships in Australian waters .

However, serious concerns about bulk carrier safety first arose much earlier in Japan, after the loss of the relatively new *Bolivar Maru* (1965/54,271dwt) of the Japan Line in 1969 and *California Maru* (1965/56,474dwt) of the Daiichi Line in 1970. Both foundered in heavy seas en route to Japan with iron ore cargoes.

Japan's Class NK and its Ministry of Transport worked together to introduce safety improvements, but the issue was spotlighted again in Japan when the NYK bulk carrier *Onomichi Maru* (1965/56,341dwt) broke in two in a storm in 1980 bound for Japan carrying coal. Japanese research after this loss did much to reveal the effects of slamming on large laden vessels in bad weather, and led the Japanese classification society to further refine its regulations relating to hull structural strength.

In Europe the high profile losses of the Yugoslav-built sister ships *Berge Istra* in 1975 and *Berge Vanga* in 1979 brought bulk carrier safety to the attention of the maritime community for the first time. Both 227,000dwt giant ore-oil carriers completed by Brodogradiliste "Uljanik" in 1972 and 1974 respectively, they were lost while carrying iron ore cargoes from Brazil to Japan after both had carried crude oil from the Arabian Gulf to Rotterdam before ballasting across the Atlantic.

Two seamen, who spent 19 days adrift on a liferaft, survived the loss of the *Berge Istra* and reported that three huge explosions in less than a minute destroyed the ship. Thirty other sailors died in the disaster, while the loss of the *Berge Vanga* – from analysis of the few traces of wreckage, also believed to be through explosion – took the lives of all 40 crew.

The loss of the two Sig. Bergesen sisters and the *Derbyshire* also focused attention on the possibility of generic faults in some combination carrier designs. The *Derbyshire* was the last in a series of six 169,000dwt sister OBOs from Swan Hunter's Haverton Hill yard, and all were dogged by structural problems.

The third, *Kowloon Bridge* (originally *English Bridge*), was also a casualty, wrecked near Baltimore, Ireland, in 1986 carrying iron ore from Sept-Iles, Quebec, to Hunterston on the Clyde. The ship had sought shelter for repairs after cracks developed in the deck.

The *Derbyshire*, completed in 1976 as the *Liverpool Bridge*, sank south of Okinawa during Typhoon Orchid in September, 1980, with the loss of 44 people. She, too, was en route from Sept-Iles, carrying iron ore concentrates to Kawasaki after a stores call off Cape Town, and her last message on September 9 reported she was hove-to in the typhoon.

It took nearly seven years before the UK Department of Transport ordered a formal investigation into the disappearance of the largest British-registered ship ever lost, and its decision in January, 1989, was that the *Derbyshire* was "probably overwhelmed by the forces of nature in Typhoon Orchid, possibly after getting beam on to wind and sea." The evidence available did not support any firmer conclusion, it said.

That did not satisfy relatives of the crew or many maritime industry professionals – especially the inquiry's dismissal of structural defects, particularly in the area of frame No.65, close to the superstructure, as a possible cause. All six ships of the class had problems with cracking there.

Public pressure led to a second inquiry by Mr Justice Colman in the High Court, which benefited from a comprehensive underwater survey of the wreck – at a depth of more than two and a half miles (4300m) – by the American Woods Hole Oceanographic Institution. The Colman report in November 2000 blamed the loss on progressive collapse of the main hatch covers and consequent flooding of the holds from No.1, after the destruction of some or all of the ventilators and airpipes on the foredeck by sustained green water loading, and flooding of the bow spaces as a result. After No.3 hatch collapsed the ship was "irretrievably lost."

Minimum hatch cover strength requirements laid down by the 1966 International Load Line Convention were "seriously deficient" for present day safety requirements, he said. And he urged the UK government to press "strongly and urgently" for new standards for minimum hatch cover strength – applicable not only to newbuildings but also to existing bulk carriers.

In the early 1990s Australia started looking closely at bulk carrier safety after the following ships were lost after sailing from West Australian ports:

• *Singa Sea* (1976/26,568dwt) Bulk carrier, Philippines flag (ex-*Dona Magdalena*, built Govan) Sailed July 2, 1988, for Rotterdam via Cape Town after loading mineral sands and copper ore at Geraldton and Bunbury. Six survivors were rescued a month later and reported the ship broke in two in heavy seas on July 4.

• *Alexandre-P* (1967/94,532 dwt) Ore-oil carrier adapted for ore only, Panama (ex-*Acacia* and *Tsurusaki Maru*, built Mitsubishi). Sailed March 13, 1990, from Dampier for Cape Town and Gijon with iron ore. Last position report March 14. Weather and sea conditions light at the time. One liferaft found March 20. The ship was reportedly not well-maintained, with heavy corrosion and wastage around the main deck and cargo hatches and in the upper sections of the transverse bulkheads between holds 2 and 3.

• *Sanko Harvest* (1985/33,024dwt) Bulk carrier, Panama (built Mitsubishi). Grounded February 14, 1991, in shoal water between Hastings and Hood Islands on passage from Tampa to Esperance with fertiliser. Crew evacuated and ship broke up and sank February 17-18.

• *Starfish* (1970/56,277dwt) Bulk carrier, Panama (ex-*Genkai Maru*, built Maizuru Jukogyo). Reflagged from Argentina flag, March 15, 1991. Sailed March 22, 1991, from Port Walcott for Swinoujscie with iron ore fines, and diverted to Port Louis April 1 with water in holds 6 and 7. Ship escorted to deep water by Mauritius Coast Guard and sank on April 8.

• *Mineral Diamond* (1982/141,028dwt). Bulk carrier, Hong Kong (ex-*Mountain Thistle*, built Hyundai). Sailed April 11, 1991, from Dampier for Ijmuiden via the Cape. Last reporting message received April 17. Ship had reduced speed in bad weather.

• *Manila Transporter* (1976/115,960dwt) Bulk carrier, Philippines (ex-*Shinsho Maru*, built Mitsubishi). Sailed June 26, 1991, from Dampier for Port Talbot with iron ore fines. Crew abandoned ship on July 7, after the ship started taking water in No.3 hold. Ship sank August 7. Lifeboats repairs made in Dampier after a port state control inspection were reported as "instrumental in the successful outcome of the abandonment" by the crew of 24.

• *Melete* (1975/72,063dwt) Bulk carrier, Greece (built Sunderland Shipbuilders). Sailed August 11, 1991, from Dampier for Port Talbot with iron ore fines. Distress call received August 24. Two survivors.

• *Daeyang Honey* (1970/123,745dwt) Ore carrier, South Korea (ex-*Yachiyosan Maru*, built Kawasaki). Sailed October 14, 1992, from Koolan Island for Mizushima with low grade iron ore. Float-free emergency position indicator radio beacon from the ship was detected October 22 about 300 miles east of the Philippines close to the area of Typhoon Colleen. One liferaft located later. No survivors.

Losses like these and the disappearance of other very large bulk carriers led authors Dave Ramwell and Tim Madge in their 1992 book "A Ship Too Far – the Mystery of the Derbyshire" to say:

"... literally hundreds of lives could have been saved, millions of tons of cargo not lost, hundreds of millions in insurance not paid out, if the lessons of the Derbyshire and many other bulk carriers had been learned earlier. Those lessons were not just about the Bridge class of ships. The bigger, broader picture is that bulk carriers, in the nature of what they are and what they do, are highly vulnerable to certain kinds of problem. One of these is slamming in heavy seas ... another is brittle fracture under certain conditions. But there are more – one authority has identified as many as 21 problems."

The Australian ore ship losses led to an Australian parliamentary enquiry chaired by Transport Minister Peter Morris. Its Ships of Shame Report was released in December 1992, and it stressed that Australia could not act alone but needed to take a more active role at the International Maritime Organisation promoting international solutions to safety issues, and to influence other nations with an interest in safety to present a united front.

The major recommendations of Ships of Shame, a wakeup call which galvanised the shipping industry worldwide to address the problems, were:

• Australian representation at the IMO be strengthened by the inclusion of industry and trade delegates with relevant experience.

• Operating criteria for classification societies to be introduced, and an IMO "seal of approval" for societies meeting the criteria.

• Improvements to Australian Maritime Safety Authority port state control inspecting (particularly at ports where substandard ships have been a problem) to the level where it ceases to be viable for substandard ships to call at Australian ports.

• AMSA to impose penalty surcharges on substandard shipping to fund the increased level of operations they generate.

• Monthly reports for port state control inspections at each port to be published, with information on the defects, ownership, flag, classification society etc of offending vessels.

• Dry bulk carriers entering Australian ports to carry a mandatory file on their survey history, and full information on the commercial chain from beneficial owner to cargo owner available to the AMSA, so that responsibility for pollution damage can be determined.

• The IMO to establish an international accreditation system for crew training and issuing of qualifications, and samples of crew qualification certificates from each flag state to be obtained by the AMSA to help determine the authenticity of documents inspected by surveyors.

• Adoption by all international shipping organisations of the IMO resolution on Guidelines for Management of Safe Ship Operations and Pollution Prevention.

• Ships not meeting International Labour Organisation standards for crew conditions to be denied entry to Australian waters.

• AMSA and IMO to create comprehensive ship information databases.

• Foreign vessels in Australian ports to have proof of adequate Protection and Indemnity insurance.

What has changed after the Colman and Morris reports? For all the discussion they prompted among seafarers, unions, shipowners groups, the International Maritime Organisation, classification societies, naval architects, and maritime commentators, some say the answer is "not enough," although port state inspections have certainly been conducted much more vigorously in countries like Australia. At least 64 bulkers and more than 670 lives were lost in the decade from 1990.

The loss with her crew of 27 of another Capesize bulker, the Cypriot *Christopher* (1983/ 164,891dwt) in the Atlantic in December, 2001, prompted Mr Justice Colman to criticize, with unusual frankness for a senior member of the UK judiciary, the lack of action since his *Derbyshire* report. Serious structural deficiencies in the *Christopher* had been exposed in a port state inspection at Ningbo, China, in 2001. The ship, ex-*Federal Skeena* and *La Cordillera* and the last ship built by NV Scheepswerven, Hoboken, was carrying coal from Puerto Bolivar to Redcar when she was lost in severe weather. Like the *Derbyshire*, she received hatch cover damage and flooded forward.

In a letter to "Lloyd's List" in January, 2002, Mr Justice Colman criticised both the International Association of Classification Societies and Lloyd's Register (which classed both the *Derbyshire* and *Christopher*) for lack of urgency in revising bulk carrier requirements.

Classification societies still had not acted to implement his recommendations for much increased hatch cover strength requirements to cover older bulk carriers. "How many more *Derbyshires* and *Christophers* will it need for the societies to get their act together?" he asked.

Nevertheless, there has been action. In 1997 the UN's International Maritime Organisation agreed to new requirements for bulk carriers 150m or more in length, as chapter 7 to the International Convention for the Safety of Life at Sea. Taking effect in July 1999, the new SOLAS regulations particularly set out to prevent the sudden catastrophic structural failures which had led to the demise of so many bulk carriers, and gave close attention to ensuring the strength of two vulnerable areas -- the transverse bulkhead between holds No.1 and 2 (the foremost cargo holds), and the double bottom in that area.

Some naval architects have been very critical of the fact so many bulk carriers, particularly large ones like the *Christopher*, are designed without a raised forecastle and hence have insufficient freeboard at the bow in heavy seas. It does not take a naval architect to realise a raised forecastle must provide advantages in buoyancy and protection when a laden bulker is butting into large waves in rough weather.

It is also argued that double hulls would make bulk carriers safer. Oshima Shipbuilding led the way in double hull construction in the 1990s, and now double hull designs are offered by many Japanese, Korean, and Chinese shipyards. Their advocates say that double hull bulk carriers better withstand collision, create stiffer side structures so eliminating flexing and fatigue where side frame and shell plating join, avoid the exposure of framing to corrosion and fatigue, offer some advantages for maintenance, and (not least), with smooth sides to the holds, also speed up cleaning and cargo handling.

Mandatory double hulls have been strongly opposed by many shipowners concerned that the value of existing single hull vessels will be reduced, as happened when double hulls were legislated for oil tankers. Greek shipowners, who operate a very large part of the dry bulk fleet, have been among the opponents, contending that more strongly built vessels and prudent seamanship are the way to improve bulk carrier safety. The Union of Greek Shipowners argued in its 2002 annual report that the longevity and robustness of ships were the real questions for bulk carriers, and these depended primarily on the scantlings, corrosion margins, and the coatings in wet spaces. And operational measures like weather routeing, reducing speed in heavy seas, and change of heading were more effective than raising the freeboard or reintroducing forecastles, it said.

Apart from the "commercial implications" and "technical problems" which double hull vessels posed, there was the prospect of "unnecessarily creating a two-tier market, with a totally unjustified bias against single hull designs," said the UGS.

In 2004 the IMO's Maritime Safety Committee controversially rejected plans to make double skins for new bulk carriers mandatory from 2007, after two years developing the new double hull regulations, for which the United Kingdom was a strong advocate.

Also under scrutiny has been structural failure in bulk carriers because of brittle fracture. A Canadian investigation into the loss of American-owned, Marshall Islands-flagged, and Turkish-built Lake Carling (1992/26,264dwt) in the lower St Lawrence River in March 2002 after the hull cracked raised concern about this. It also revealed that 23 bulk carriers had been lost in cold water in 20 years, and expressed concern about the quality of some of the steel used in the construction of the Lake Carling.

Aside from safety considerations, bulk carriers have come under increasing attention for environmental hazards. Once it was wrecked tankers that caused alarm and featured prominently in television news clips and on the front page of newspapers. Now bulk carriers are also under the microscope – not helped by a lamentable knack for making the headlines with high profile mishaps.

In New Zealand (a maritime country very sensitive to environmental issues), for example, they have been at the centre of a series of spectacular accidents in recent years. In February 1999 the Panamanian woodchip carrier Prince of Tokyo (1997/43,980dwt) was aground for two days at the north mole at Port Chalmers as environmentalists seethed about the risk to the famous albatross colony nearby if her bunker tanks ruptured.

In 2002 two loggers got unwanted national attention and also caused pollution alerts with mishaps on the front doorsteps of two port-towns. The Panamanian Jody F Millennium (2000/25,369dwt) was aground at popular Waikanae beach, Gisborne, for 18 days in February, and then the Hong Kong-flagged Tai Ping (1997/26,411dwt) aground at Bluff harbour for nine days in October.

And in November 2003 it was the turn of Port Chalmers for another alarm over bulk carriers when a crane broke off its pedestal while another Hong Kong bulker, the Maritime Friendship (1984/29,135dwt), was loading logs. Several days earlier more than half of the ship's stanchions had been condemned after two broke during loading.

The biggest bulk carrier operating in New Zealand waters, the Panamanian iron sand carrier Taharoa Express (1990/145,842dwt) blotted her copybook twice, being disabled in March 2003 off the Northland coast when a crack was discovered in her propeller shaft, and then being deemed a "hazardous ship" and ordered to stay 40 miles offshore by the NZ Maritime Safety Authority in February 2004 when her engine failed as she was approaching the Taharoa offshore loading buoy. The enormous ship was in the surf zone before she could be anchored.

On top of these mishaps, yet another bulk carrier, the Athena (1995/28,458dwt), was blamed when stocks of cornflour and babyfood had to be pulled off the country's supermarket shelves in 2004 because they were contaminated with lead. The contamination was attributed to the ship, which had carried a coastal cargo of lead concentrate in Australia before shipping the corn from Dalian to Auckland a voyage or two later.

If fears of pollution in the New Zealand accidents proved unfounded, some other countries have not been so fortunate. The loss of the Philippine-flag woodchip carrier New Carissa (1989/44,529dwt) at Coos Bay, Oregon, in 1999 required expenditure of more than US$30 million to clean up the oil spill that resulted, and in huge claims for compensation.

Even countries not noted for environmental awareness have become more sensitive to maritime accidents. Taiwan suffered damage to the coral reefs in a national park when oil leaked from the Greek bulk carrier Amorgos (1984/65,105dwt) after she was wrecked in 2001, and a year later announced it would seek more than US$28 million in compensation from the owners.

Australia had an environmental scare when the Greek bulk carrier Doric Chariot (1994/73,350dwt) ran aground on a sandbank near the Great Barrier Reef in 2002 – while under pilotage.

It does not need an accident for the bulk carrier master and his ship to be targeted by environmentalists. Concerns about the spread of harmful organisms – including crabs, starfish, jellyfish, kelp, toxic algae, and even cholera – in some parts of the world through ballast water discharges has had bulk carriers under particular suspicion. At least three billion tonnes of water ballast are moved every year, and the IMO has tackled this issue industriously in the past 10 years or so. In 2004 the International Convention for the Control and Management of Ships' Ballast Water and Sediments was adopted, requiring all ships to implement a Ballast Water and Sediments Management Plan.

If that extra paperwork – and let's not forget all the security measures in the wake of September 11 and the requirements of the International Ship and Port Facility Security Code introduced in July 2004 – isn't enough for the harassed bulk carrier master, he also has to be ready to repel environmental boarders as organisations like Greenpeace extend their concerns about genetically-modified crops to making protest raids on bulk carriers. That's happened in Australia, Britain, France, Denmark, Canada, Brazil, and other countries.

However, that pales against what the crew of the bulk carrier Nisha (1977/27,481dwt), owned by one of India's major companies, Great Eastern Shipping Co, suffered at the end of 2001 when intelligence bumbling led to the ship being intercepted in the English Channel by the frigate HMS Sutherland and boarded by anti-terrorist police, the navy, and customs personnel. Instead of the "terrorist material" they were seeking, they found 26,000 tonnes of raw sugar destined for Tate & Lyle's London refinery.

However, among the reports of disaster and calamity, there is occasionally one with a lighter side. The Maltese bulker Kouros V (1983/25,449dwt) provided one in 2001 when she joined the Ignominious list of ships to have struck lighthouses, colliding with the Ambrose Tower in the New York harbour approaches in the early hours of the morning.

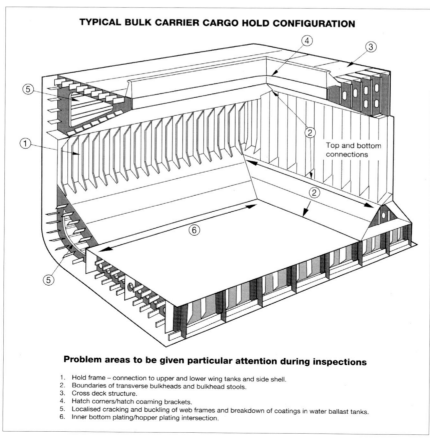

TYPICAL BULK CARRIER CARGO HOLD CONFIGURATION

Top and bottom connections

Problem areas to be given particular attention during inspections

1. Hold frame – connection to upper and lower wing tanks and side shell.
2. Boundaries of transverse bulkheads and bulkhead stools.
3. Cross deck structure.
4. Hatch corners/hatch coaming brackets.
5. Localised cracking and buckling of web frames and breakdown of coatings in water ballast tanks.
6. Inner bottom plating/hopper plating intersection.

Preventing structural failure: The problem areas to be targeted in inspections, from an International Association of Classification Societies pamphlet for shipowners. (IACS/Class NK)

Berge Vanga – General Ore International Corporation (Sig. Bergesen d.y. & Co), Liberia; Brodogradiliste "Uljanik," Pula, 1973; 227,561dwt, 314m, 10ha, 35,000bhp 2 x Brodogradiliste-B&W. (World Ship Society)

Two of the many bulk carriers to go missing: The loss of the ore-oil carrier *Berge Vanga* (above) in 1979 after her sister *Berge Istra* in 1975 focussed attention on the safety of combination carriers. The 12-year-old Indian ship *Kairali*, pictured below as she was originally as the 21,550dwt Norwegian *Saga Sword*, is one in the toll of smaller bulker carriers lost. With a crew of 51, she disappeared in the Arabian Sea in July 1979 bound from Mormugao to Rostock with iron ore, via Djibouti for bunkers.

Saga Sword – I/S Saga Sword (Ole Schroder & Co), Norway; Marinens Hovedverft, Horten, 1967; 21,550dwt, 160m, 6ha, 6 x 8tn cr, 9600bhp Sulzer. (Tolerton)

The 1980 loss of the *Derbyshire,* built as the *Liverpool Bridge* and the largest British ship ever lost, was a wake-up call over bulk carrier safety. (*Liverpool Bridge* photo, World Ship Society)

Ocean Bridge – Bibby Line, UK; Sumitomo, Yokosuka, 1970; 113,370dwt, 259m, 9ha, 25,000bhp Sumitomo-Sulzer. (APN)

Bibby's Japanese-built OBO *Ocean Bridge* required the most extensive repairs performed at a British shipyard after an explosion in an aft hold in the Bay of Biscay in March 1971 (above). The master was killed in the accident, and the ship was out of service until December 1972 when repairs at a Clyde yard were completed. The new 136,400dwt Italian ore-oil carrier *Igara*, laden with Brazilian iron ore for Japan via the Sunda Strait, joined the long list of bulker casualties when she hit an uncharted rock in the South China Sea in March 1973 (below) to become the most expensive single marine insurance loss to that time. The afterpart was salvaged and rebuilt into a new vessel, the *Eraclide*.

Igara – Pluto SpA di Nav, Italy; Italcantieri, Monfalcone, 1972; 136,400dwt, 297m. (APN)

REPRESENTATIVE VOYAGES – FROM COAL AND GRAIN TO COBBLESTONES AND CKDS

The variety of cargoes carried by handysize bulk carriers is shown in this list of voyages in the 1980s and 1990s by ships operating in the Danish J Lauritzen group's bulk carrier pool:

Vitina, soyabeans, Great Lakes to Valencia and Sevilla.

Righteous, fertiliser, Tampa, Florida, to Prescott and Hamilton, Ontario (first St Lawrence Seaway vessel of the season).

Han Pacific, fluorspar, Tampico, Mexico, to Windsor, Ontario.

Nordic Trader, cement, Montreal to New Orleans.

Menhir, fluorspar, Tampico to Windsor (first St Lawrence Seaway vessel of the season).

Arctic Trader, sulphur, Vancouver to Finland (maiden voyage after completion in Japan).

Copenhagen Maru, bauxite, Guyana to Hamilton, Ontario, and Gary, Indiana.

Drava, petroleum coke, Port Arthur, Texas, to Becancour, Canada.

Adriatic Trader, coal, Rotterdam to Glasgow.

Nordic Trader, barley, Duluth, Minnesota, to Cartagena, Colombia.

Alaska Trader, coal, Norfolk, Virginia, to Cardiff.

Skaw Trader, pig iron, Sorel, Canada, to Bilbao.

Alaska Trader, cement, Eleusis, Greece, to Port Newark, New Jersey.

Baltic Trader, pyrites, Huelva, Spain, and gypsum, Safi, Morocco, to Owendo, Gabon.

Baltic Trader, rutile sand, Sherbro River, Sierra Leone, to Ashtabula, Ohio.

Adriatic Trader, petroleum coke, Wilmington, Delaware, to Rotterdam.

Jade Kim, gypsum, Dominican Republic to Cartagena, Colombia.

Baltic Trader, rutile sand, Sherbro River to Savannah, Georgia.

Astoria Trader, alumina, Port Esquivel, Jamaica, to Blyth.

Bothnia Trader, gypsum, Safi, Morocco, to Abidjan, Ivory Coast.

Skaw Trader, urea, Point Lisas, Trinidad, to Donaldsonville, Louisiana.

Atlantic Trader 1, debarked pine logs, Lirquen, Chile, to Turkey.

Freesia, lumber, US North Pacific to New York and US east coast ports.

Anangel Success, coal, Sydney, Nova Scotia, to Copenhagen.

Jade Kim, coal, Venezuela to Germany.

Baltic Trader, fertiliser, Glomfjord, Norway, to Essexville, Michigan.

Fidestar, scrap, USA to Orinoco River, Venezuela.

Ambar, steel products, Germany to US Gulf ports.

Viking Trader, fertiliser, Sluiskil, Holland, to Charlottetown, Prince Edward Island.

Camara, limestone, Lake Maracaibo, Venezuela, to Matanzas, Venezuela.

Arctic Trader, cement, Mylaki, Greece, to Port Everglades, Florida, and Freeport, Bahamas.

Atlantic Trader 1, cement clinker, Vassiliko Bay, Cyprus, to Fort de France, Martinique.
Nordic Trader, ilmenite, Sherbro River to New Orleans.
Atlantic Trader 1, ilmenite and rutile sand, Sherbro River to New Orleans and Antioch.
Baltic Trader, petroleum coke, US Gulf to Porto Marghera, Italy.
William, alumina, Paranam, Surinam, and Rocky Point, Jamaica, to Rotterdam.
Atlahua, cement clinker, Poland to Rio Haina, Dominican Republic.
Arctic Trader, cement, Le Havre to New Orleans.
Berta Dan, steel ingot, Brazil to Contrecouer, Quebec, and Hamilton, Ontario.
Dan Bauta, mineral sand, Australia, to Port Weller and Ashtabula.
Dania Portland, white cement, Aalborg, Denmark, to Florida.
Atlantic Trader 1, chemical grade salt, Bonaire to Port Newark.
Bella Dan, cement, Le Havre to New Orleans.
Berta Dan, coal, New Orleans to Kingston, Jamaica.
Magnolia, lead and zinc ore, Maarmorilik, Greenland, to Nordenham, Germany.
William, coal, Sydney, Nova Scotia, to Copenhagen.
Bella Dan, coal, Puerto Prodeco, Colombia, to Italy.
Camara, coal, Newport News, Virginia, to Spain.
Federal St. Laurent, fertiliser, Tampa to Contrecouer.
Alaska Trader, cement, Cumarebo, Venezuela, to El Palito, Venezuela.
Kristianiafjord, phosphate, Tampa to Landskrona, Sweden.
Nirja, fertiliser, Landskrona to Chiwan, China.
Centa Dan, gravel, Fujairah, UAE, to Male, the Maldives.
Shine Ho, aluminium ingots, Brazil to Liverpool (largest shipment of this cargo imported into UK).
Berta Dan, bauxite, Takoradi, Ghana, to St Lawrence River.
Pingwo Venture, coal, Guanta, Venezuela, to Hull.
Bijelo Polje, corn, New Orleans to Durban, South Africa, and Beira, Mozambique.
Berta Dan, coke breeze, Canada to Antwerp.
Celia Dan, manganese ore, Takoradi, Ghana, to Kvinesdal, Norway
Atlas, petcoke, New Orleans to Safaga, Egypt.
Atlantis II, aggregates, Norway to Sicily for offshore ship-to-ship discharge to pipe-laying vessel near Trapani.
Dobrush, colemanite, Bandirma, Turkey, to Charleston.
Dania Portland, alumina, Port Kaiser, Jamaica, to Norway.
Dobrush, potash, St John, New Brunswick, to Fredericia, Denmark.
Regina Oldendorff, petroleum coke, US Gulf to Vassiliko Bay, Cyprus.
Muriel, manganese ore, South Africa to Porsgrunn, Norway.
Sea Ace, soybean meal, Mississippi River, and fish meal, Ilo, Peru, to Lyttelton, New Plymouth, and Auckland, New Zealand, and Brisbane and Melbourne, Australia.
Diamond Bulker, CKDs (cars knocked-down), Japan to Sydney and Melbourne, Australia (maiden voyage), then ilmenite, Bunbury, Western Australia, to Spain, then cement clinker, Huelva to Puerto Plata, Dominican Republic.
Aston Trader, bulk and bagged limestone, to Takoradi, then bauxite, Takoradi to Port Alfred, Quebec.
Marianna, cement clinker, Pertigalete, Venezuela, to Port Manatee, Florida.
Baltic Confidence, manganese ore, Santana, Brazil, to Antwerp.
Baltic Bulker, cement clinker, San Marcos Island, to Tolu, Colombia, and Cumarebo, Venezuela.
Sailman, limestone, Newfoundland, to Point Lisas, Trinidad.
Nedi, rice, New Orleans to Paranagua, Brazil.
Baltic Bulker, eucalyptus logs, Concepcion del Uruguay and Campana, Argentina, to Pasajes, Spain.
Caribbean Bulker, steel products, four Japanese ports, to Sydney, Geelong, and Adelaide, Australia, then steel products, Westernport and Newcastle, Australia, to South East Asia.
Svitava, cement clinker, Nador, Morocco, to Abidjan.
Skaw Bulker, alumina, Geraldton, Western Australia, to Rotterdam (maiden voyage).

Crystal Bulker, wheat, Vancouver to Recife and Rio de Janeiro (maiden voyage).

Atlantic Bulker, cement clinker, Pertigalete, Venezuela, to Martinique and Guadeloupe.

Artemon and *Diamond Bulker*, cement clinker, Venezuela to Conchan, Peru.

Emerald Bulker, logs, Tauranga, New Zealand to Far East.

Nordic Bulker, coal, Barranquilla, Colombia, to Salaverry, Peru.

Skaw Bulker, sawn timber, Breves and Vila do Conde, Brazil, to Durban, Bangkok, Manila.

Crystal Bulker, eucalyptus logs, Concepcion del Uruguay and Montevideo to Pasajes, Spain.

Lilac Wave, ilmenite, Australia to Tahkoluoto, Finland, then scrap metal, Mantyluoto and Kotka, Finland, to Malaysia.

Kissamos Wave, coal, South Africa to Aalborg, Denmark, then rapeseed, Poland to west coast Mexico.

Diamond Bulker, debarked pine logs, Guanta, Venezuela, to Viana do Castelo, Portugal.

Yue Hai, phosphate, Aqaba, Jordan, to Rotterdam.

Tai Ping Ying, mineral sand, Western Australia to Tyssedal, Norway.

Viking Bulker, grain, Australia to Hodeidah, Yemen.

Sea Rose, iron ore pellets, Tubarao, Brazil, to Tampico.

Nan Hai, scrap, Gdansk, Poland, to South East Asian ports.

Sea Rose, bauxite, Takoradi to Port Alfred, Canada.

Skaw Bulker, pine logs, New Zealand ports finishing Nelson to South East Asia.

Pretty Flourish, ilmenite, Bunbury, Western Australia, to Tyssedal, Norway.

Emerald Bulker, pig iron, Ponta da Madeira, Brazil, to Charleston, South Carolina.

Vamand Wave, cobblestones, Madras, India, to Port Newark, then coal, Norfolk, Virginia, to England.

Orhan Deval, copper concentrate, Caleta Coloso, Chile, to Asia.

Viking Bulker, logs and woodchips, Tallinn, Estonia, to Viana do Castelo, Portugal.

Orhan Deval, wheat, Vancouver to Callao, Peru, and Antofagasta, Chile.

Salusnavis, mineral sand, Geraldton, and lead and zinc concentrates, King Sound, Western Australia, to USA.

Glorious Sun, shredded scrap, Malmoe, Sweden, to Charleston, South Carolina.

Tong Shan Hai, garnet sands and talc, Geraldton, and lead and zinc concentrates, Derby, Western Australia, to Norfolk and New Orleans.

Great Motion, fertiliser, Vancouver, Canada, and Portland, Oregon, to Geraldton.

Bei Hai, ilmenite, Geraldton to Altamira, Mexico, and Gulfport, Mississippi.

Hudson Trader, cement clinker, Bizerta, Tunisia, to Santa Cruz, Tenerife.

Viking Bulker, phosphate, Nauru to Napier, Whangarei, Lyttelton, and Dunedin, New Zealand, then logs, Napier and Tauranga, to South Korea.

Pacific Bulker, urea, Bintulu, Malaysia, to Melbourne, then wheat, Adelaide to India.

Erikousa Wave, urea, Riga, Latvia, to Peru.

Hudson Trader (1997/28,500dwt), a standard design from Kanasashi. (Tolerton)

HEADACHES OF THE BULK CARRIER MASTER

Like tankermen, those who man bulk carriers sometimes have reason to feel they are the forgotten men of shipping. The lament of a Bibby master, Captain Peter Boyle, in a paper to a Nautical Institute conference on Port Facilities and the Mariner in 1979 would still strike chords today.

On traffic management: "This varies from the very sophisticated management of some of the North European ports to the virtually nonexistent management of some ports in the emergent nations....there are ports in other parts of the world where one knows before arrival that there will be a fight to berth the ship. In a recent experience of mine I was delayed for two hours at the entrance to a harbour because dredges were obstructing the fairway. Eventually the dredgers moved, but not until there had been a four-way argument on Channel 16 between the dredger, the pilot of my ship, the consignee, and my agent. The Harbourmaster did not seem to be interested. I subsequently discovered that the dredging company had a contract to fulfill by a certain date and that they did not really care that they were stopping the operation of the port. I think that in this case it is fair to say that traffic management did not exist."

On pilotage: "Here is another aspect of port operations which varies greatly throughout the world. The skill of the pilot, however, does not vary directly with the sophistication of the port. I have witnessed some very impressive displays of ship-handling skills in some of the small ore ports on the west coast of South America where single screw ships of 80,000 to 120,000 tonnes are berthed very snugly in some of the exposed open bays without the use of tugs."

On stevedores and terminal operations: "Why do stevedore companies always use their greenest trainee grab drivers to discharge my ship? There are extraordinary amounts of damage on occasions. A recent experience of mine involved the piercing of bunker tanks by the discharging grabs....There are some ports where the stevedores will not even acknowledge that any damage has been done, whilst in others, despite the fact that the foreman will acknowledge by signing the damage report that damage has been done, they will neither repair the damage, nor, my head office tells me, will they pay for the damage when it is eventually made good at some subsequent port....In most loading ports in the world I have found the terminal operators to be very co-operative. I wonder at their patience sometimes because the loading of a large bulk carrier might require as many as 30 rig shifts for nine holds. This is necessary, of course, to avoid unacceptable stresses in the ship. Having said that, however, I have known the nightshift rig operator to fall asleep and load much more than was asked for in a particular hold."

Port documentation and clearance: "There is a great diversity between the clearing procedures not only of different countries but also of different ports in the same country....sometimes the authorities in one port do not know which documents the authorities in the next port within the same country will require. One port in the world requires no less than 10 crew lists, plus two which should have been posted from the previous country....There are some countries which insist that all information is given on their standard forms. This can be a problem if the ship does not carry a supply of blank forms and clearance can be held up for a number of hours until the correct information is given on the standard forms. Some countries require visaed crew lists attested by an officer of their embassy at the last port of call, whilst others even require a visaed bonded stores list. Cargo manifests must arrive by mail at least eight days before the arrival of the ship at one port in one of the African countries."

Gangways: "A frequently recurring problem....some ports do supply a substantial platform for easy access to the foot of the gangway. Most do not, however, with the result that the foot of the accommodation ladder has to be landed on the quay. The quay, due to heavy fendering and the curve of the ship's hull at the quarter, can be as much as 12 feet from the foot of the accommodation ladder hanging vertically beneath the accommodation ladder davit. In order to land the ladder on the quay, it is necessary to disconnect it from the bridle, and at many ports there is a considerable surge in the harbour, so that the foot of the ladder is constantly moving on the quay and at risk from bollards, railway lines, and ring bolts. The ideal would be to have a shore gangway, as there is in many tanker ports. Undoubtedly, however, the people who operate the ore terminals consider that it is not worth providing a shore gangway as there is no financial return for doing so."

Agents: "...can really be divided into two main groups, owners' agents and charterers' agents. When I was a cadet in the old regular liner trades, one of the most important jobs which the agent had, to my inexperienced eyes, was to ensure that there was a car available to take the 'Old Man' to the golf club. In those days the owners' agent knew the ships, the masters, the owners, shippers, and consignees very intimately and the agency had probably served the company for more than 50 years....Today, with many ships consigned to charterers' agents, the master's lot is frequently not a happy one. It is understandable that an agent will show more allegiance to a charterer who has perhaps as many as 50 ships per year arriving at a port than he will to any individual ships which belong to different owners."

Difficult situations: "The most difficult situation of recent years is the 'quart into a pint pot' situation....understandably, everyone within the industry is trying to maximise his returns on cargo carried. Whilst I can understand the motives, I do not believe that it is very wise. There are a number of places in particular which spring to mind when considering this problem – the Mississippi River, the Sabine River, Weipa in Queensland, Jebel Dhanna, and Port Cartier. The problem of the big ship in a small port is not confined to depth of water, but is also concerned with the width of channels and physical dimensions of the port. There is absolutely no safety margin when taking a 247m long by 32m beam ship along a seven mile channel which is only 91m wide. When steering to counter a current setting across the channel, virtually the whole width of the channel is occupied by the ship. Another problem encountered by bulk carriers is the lack of tugs of adequate power in so many of the world's ports. I have noticed that tanker ports generally seem to be well supplied with tugs. Trying to berth a vessel displacing 100,000 tons with the aid of one 1000hp tug can have some heart-stopping moments."

Desirable facilities: "A very difficult problem in many parts of the world is the loading of stores. In some ports it is impossible for the lorry delivering the stores to get near the ship....It is common these days for ships to load, say, six months' stores at one time. This can only be achieved with the expenditure of a considerable number of man hours, 170 for the last storing that I did, and this was only to load the stores and distribute them roughly about the ship....At one port which I know, stores have to be wheeled down a narrow catwalk about 260m long on a small wheeled trolley, providing the ship can supply one. At another port, packing cases have to be opened on the ship chandler's tuck and all spares carried by hand to the ship because the truck cannot approach closer than 150m to the ship. If the truck could drive under the stores derrick, the spare parts could be loaded with two lifts."

4
2
14 M
8
6
4
2
13 M
8
6
4
2
12 M
8
6
4
2
11 M
8
6
4
2
10 M
8
6
4
2
9 M
8
6
4
2
8 M
8
6
4
2
7 M
8
6
4
2
6 M
8
6
4

BIBLIOGRAPHY AND ACKNOWLEDGEMENTS

Lloyd's Register *Register of Ships*, Class NK *Register*, World Ship Society *Marine News*, NZ Ship & Marine Society *Marine News*, *The Motor Ship*, *Ships Monthly*, *Sea Breezes*, *Fairplay*, *Lloyds List*, Hawke's Bay NZS&MS *Leading Lights*, *Bluff Portsider*.

Appleyard H, *Turnbull Scott & Co*; Australian House of Representatives Transport Committee, *Ships of Shame Report*; Bakka D, *Hoegh, Shipping through Cycles*; Clark R, Lindsay R, Robertson D, *The Australian National Line 1956-81*; Clarkson J, Fenton R, *Ships in Focus Record*, Clarkson J, Harvey B, Fenton R, *Blue Funnel Line*; Cubbin G, *Harrisons of Liverpool*; Dear I, *The Ropner Story*; Detlefsen G, *75 Years, The Ships of Egon Oldendorff*; Dick H, Kentwell S, *Beancaker to Boxboat*; Dunn L, *Merchant Ships 1910-29*; Ewart W, *Bulk Carriers*; Firth P, *A Class Act, The History of Class NK*; Gage N, *Hellas A Portrait of Greece*; Gray L, *H Hogarth & Sons*; Harlaftis G, *A History of Greek-Owned Shipping*, Harlaftis, *Greek Shipowners and Greece 1945-75*; Harvey W, *Hadley*; Heal S, *The Maple Leaf Afloat Vol.2*; Heaton P, *Reardon Smith*; Hirsimaki E, *The Lakers Vol.1*; Hooke N, *Modern Shipping Disasters 1963-87*; International Association of Classification Societies, brochures; Japan Ship Exporters' Association, *Shipbuilding & Marine Engineering in Japan*; Jenkins D, *The Golden Cross Line*; Kummerman H, Jacquinet R, *Ships' Cargo, Cargo Ships*; Lingwood J, *Significant Ships*; Lingwood J, Appleyard H, *Chapman of Newcastle*; Long A & R, *A Shipping Venture, Turnbull Scott & Co*; Mallett A, *Idyll of the Kings*; Mitsui OSK, *The First Century of Mitsui OSK Lines*; Musk G, *Canadian Pacific*; NYK Line, *Voyage of a Century*; Orbell J, *From Cape to Cape, the History of Lyle Shipping*; Paget-Tomlinson E, *Bibby Line, 175 Years of Achievement*; Rabson S, O'Donoghue K, *P&O, A Fleet History*; Ramwell D, Madge T, *A Ship Too Far, the Mystery of the Derbyshire*; Riley D, Crisp D, *The Iron Ships, A Maritime History of BHP*; Rinman T, *The Johnson Line*; Robinson N, *Stag Line*; Scott R, *Standard Ship Designs, Bulk Carriers & Tankers*; Sedgwick S, Sprake R, *London & Overseas Freighters*; Silver Line, *Half a Century of Silver Line*; Somner G, *Ben Line*; Spong H, *Irish Shipping*; Transport (UK), Dept of, *MV Derbyshire Report*; Vodena-Mitsiou M, *10,000 Years of Greek shipping Vol.2*; Watson N, *The Bibby Line*; Williams M, MacDonald B, *The Phosphateers*.

Australasian Ships & Ports, *Lauritzen News*, *Denholm News*, *Bibby Gazette*, *Harrison Line Newsletter*, *Silver Line Newsletter*, *Christchurch Star*, *Timaru Herald*.

The websites of Equasis, Skaarup Shipping, Scottish Ship Management, International Maritime Organisation, Intercargo, International Transport Workers' Federation, Australian Transport Safety Bureau, Maritime Safety Authority of NZ, and various shipping companies and shipyards were also helpful in the compiling of this book.

I am grateful to several individuals for valuable assistance, in particular Captain Michael Pryce, photographers Kees Lous of Ijmuiden and Kevin Moore of Durban, and Bob Anderson and Tristan Brehaut of Willson Scott Publishing. Also Markus Berger, Marcelo Lopes, Barbara Jones (Lloyd's Register), the Hon Peter Morris, Zoe Reynolds, Noboru Uchiyama, Aiden McCabe, Amitava Chatterjee, David Whiteside, Mason and Everard Tolerton, and the always helpful and ever patient staff of Christchurch Library.

INDEX

IMC's Malaysian-flag *Selendang Ayu* (1998/72,937dwt) wrecked in the Aleutians in December 2004. The risk of fuel oil spills in accidents like this in environmentally-sensitive areas has made bulk carrier safety receive closer attention. (Alaska Department of Fish & Game)